STAR of WONDER

STAR of WONDER

AN ADVENT DEVOTIONAL
TO ILLUMINATE THE PEOPLE, PLACES,
AND PURPOSE OF THE FIRST CHRISTMAS

Angela Hunt

BETHANYHOUSE
a division of Baker Publishing Group
Minneapolis, Minnesota

Published by Bethany House Publishers
Minneapolis, Minnesota
www.bethanyhouse.com

Bethany House Publishers is a division of
Baker Publishing Group, Grand Rapids, Michigan

Printed in the United States of America

ISBN 978-0-7642-4176-5 (cloth)
ISBN 978-1-4934-4385-7 (ebook)
Library of Congress Cataloging-in-Publication Control Number: 2023016587

Cover design and interior illustrations by Stephen Crotts

Author is represented by Browne & Miller Literary Associates.

Baker Publishing Group publications use paper produced from sustainable forestry
practices and post-consumer waste whenever possible.

23   24   25   26   27   28   29   7   6   5   4   3   2   1

For Jim Whitmire, Derric Johnson, and Gordon Luff

You three have invested in so many lives.
Thank you for investing in mine.

CONTENTS

INTRODUCTION

When we are children, the Christmas season is usually sprinkled with fairy dust and scented with cinnamon. We count the days and camp in front of the Christmas tree, anticipating the hour when we'll be allowed to open presents and see if our heartfelt wishes have come true.

Our modern Christmas features baby Jesus and Nativity scenes, holiday music and crowded malls, shiny presents and houses festooned with lights. We've heard the Christmas story dozens of times and we know each character's part: Mary had the baby, Joseph stood guard, the shepherds came to visit, and the three wise men brought gifts.

Traditions have preserved the Nativity story in pristine simplicity, but what was that first Christmas *really* like?

After writing several novels set in first-century Judea, I've discovered several practical and theological insights about the reality of the Savior's birth, and those realizations have opened my eyes to the divine majesty surrounding the people, places, promises, and purposes of Christmas. As you prayerfully contemplate this collection of readings, I hope your sense of wonder will be reignited just as mine was.

Rejoice! Unto us a child is born!

Angela Hunt

PART 1

THE PLACES OF CHRISTMAS

:1:

BETHLEHEM

We've all seen the images depicting Mary and Joseph's journey to the City of David. Mary is usually riding a donkey, with Joseph patiently leading the way as they travel through a desolate wilderness.

But what would that journey *really* have looked like?

Nazareth and Jerusalem were seventy-five miles apart, while Bethlehem was five miles farther south. Though their journey may not have been an easy one, it was far from lonely.

Back in the first century, people traveled in groups both for safety and companionship. Remember the account of twelve-year-old Jesus at the Temple? Mary and Joseph began the trip home, assuming Jesus had joined the large group from Nazareth.

Since Joseph was from Bethlehem, it's possible that some of his relatives would also be traveling to Bethlehem to register for the tax. Traveling together meant protection from bandits and mishaps. A couple traveling alone was asking for trouble.

As for that donkey, according to Fred Wright, "If Joseph had taken the position ascribed to him by many artists, of walking beside a donkey carrying Mary, he would have been the laugh-ingstock of his contemporaries."[1] Why? Because in those days, women—even pregnant women—lived to serve men, not the other way around.

Though people occasionally rode a donkey, the beasts usually carried food and water for the journey. If a heavily pregnant woman was traveling to Bethlehem with only one donkey, she would have walked or ridden in a wagon. While the thought of trudging eighty miles is enough to exhaust most of us, people in the first century were accustomed to walking such long dis-tances. Only wealthy people and Romans owned horses, while a working-class merchant might ride a mule and use a donkey to pull a cart or carry provisions.

Though the Jews hated the Roman occupation, the Romans *had* made travel easier. They paved the roads, making travel not only safer but also faster. An average family could usually cover ten miles a day. A single man could travel twenty miles if he wasn't slowed by companions, animals, or other circumstances.

What circumstances? The Romans had the right of way. When a Roman chariot or lone horseman came riding up behind a group, civilians had to leave the road and let the Romans pass. This did nothing to improve relations between Romans and Jews. Can you imagine having to pull your wagon, women, children, and pack animals off the road while an impatient Roman officer drove by?

Tax collectors also set up shop along the road, especially dur-ing pilgrimage festivals. If you were transporting crops or ani-mals, they could detain you and levy a tax on the spot.

Given these circumstances and the length of their journey, Mary and Joseph likely needed more than a week to reach Bethlehem, and they would have rested on the Sabbath.

With so many people returning home for the tax enrollment, naturally there was "no room for them in the inn" (Luke 2:7). Bethlehem probably didn't even have an inn. The Greek word translated as *inn* is *katalyma* (kah-TAL-ee-ma). The katalyma was a guest room in a private home.

The Jews considered hospitality a *mitzvah* (command) and so, upon arriving in another Jewish town, travelers would go to the city center and wait for someone to invite them to stay. Bethlehem was filled to the brim when Mary and Joseph arrived. Families would already have people sleeping in their guest rooms.

So where did Mary and Joseph find shelter? Most first-century houses had two stories—three if you count the katalyma on the flat roof. The family kept livestock on the ground floor—such as a donkey, a goat, and chickens, all of which could wander from the stable to the courtyard as they pleased—while the family lived upstairs. When guests arrived, they were escorted to the roof where they would sleep in the katalyma.

Luke tells us that Mary "gave birth to her first child, a son. She wrapped him in strips of cloth and laid him in a feeding trough, because there was no place for them in the guest quarters" (Luke 2:7 ISV). Where was the feeding trough? On the ground floor in the sheltered stable area.

Once Joseph and Marry arrived in Bethlehem, they most likely went directly to a relative's house or waited at the town center for someone to offer them shelter. Then they moved to a house and settled down with the animals because the katalyma was occupied. This is why the Son of God spent His first hours in a manger.

Someone in the house might have supplied the strips of cloth for swaddling the infant. A woman in the home probably assisted with the birth. Joseph must have spent the night pacing upstairs or in the street as the women served Mary.

But after the birth, as the house quieted and Mary rested, a group of ritually unclean shepherds left their fields and slipped into the city, going from house to house in the dark, peering over low courtyard walls as they searched for a swaddled baby in a manger.

They found Him because they sought Him.

I wonder if the people upstairs knew what had happened beneath the floorboards. Did they sense angels around the house? Did they know that all of creation had waited thousands of years for that baby's first cry?

Little Bethlehem had learned to expect the unexpected.

Bethlehem, *house of bread*, became the birthplace of One who would call himself the Bread of Life.

In Bethlehem, Ruth had married Boaz, and she, a Gentile, became the great-grandmother of King David.

In Bethlehem, Samuel the prophet found David and anointed the youngest of Jesse's sons to be king over Israel.

In Bethlehem, Mary gave birth to Jesus, the One who would sit on the throne of David forever.

The City of David, the tiny town outside Jerusalem, was never too small to host great events.

And no person is ever too insignificant to do great things for God.

A Moment for Wonder

Have you ever felt God calling you to do something, but then thought yourself too ordinary to attempt the task? You wouldn't be alone. When God called Moses to deliver His people from Egypt, Moses had a list of excuses. When God called Gideon to fight the enemies of Israel, Gideon asked for a miraculous sign— twice! Many who sat under Jesus' teaching found excuses to avoid following Him.

But Mary didn't hesitate to accept God's call. And once Joseph, her fiancé, understood the true nature of their situation, he didn't quibble. Even the shepherds, who could have dismissed the angels' news and stayed to guard their sheep, hurried out to seek the newborn Savior.

What is God calling you to do during this holiday season? Open your home to someone who's lonely? Share a meal? Reconcile with a former friend? Call that family member you haven't seen in years?

The most valuable thing you can give anyone is *time*. Your lifespan consists of a finite number of minutes, and how you invest your minutes matters greatly to God.

Father, how would you like us to invest our lives this month? Who needs us? Who is lonely? Who might enjoy spending time with us? Which ministry could use a helping hand? Show us what we can do, Lord, because Christmas isn't about us—it's about giving our time, our lives, to those you love.

2

THE GARDEN

Most people would say Christmas began in Bethlehem. But from a biblical perspective, Christmas began in Eden, otherwise known as "the Garden of God."

You're probably familiar with the story. In six days, God created light out of darkness, the sun, moon, and stars, land and sea, plants and animals, and finally, a man and a woman. Out of all the created beings, only Adam, the first man, and Eve, the first woman, were created in God's image, just as all their descendants would be. That doesn't mean we *look* like God, for He is invisible Spirit, or that only humans *think* or *feel* like God, because animals think and feel emotion, too.

Being created in God's image means we are His image-bearers or *representatives*. Just as the Roman army carried a golden image of the Roman eagle into every battle, we carry God's image into every earthly transaction.

The Lord planted a garden in the East, and He put Adam and Eve in it. Every desirable tree was in the garden, and every tree with food fit for eating.

Two other trees lived at the center of this garden: the Tree of Life and the Tree of the Knowledge of Good and Evil. We don't know what those trees looked like, but eating from the Tree of Life bestowed life. Eating from the Tree of the Knowledge of Good and Evil bestowed knowledge . . . of evil. Adam had known nothing but *good* since his first breath because everything God made was good.

God gave Adam the responsibility of cultivating and managing the garden, yet He included a warning: "From all the trees of the garden you are most welcome to eat. But of the Tree of the Knowledge of Good and Evil you must not eat. For when you eat from it, you most assuredly will die!" (Genesis 2:16–17).

Was the fruit poisonous? No. The forbidden tree could have borne apples or oranges or pomegranates. Death would not come from the tree, but from the act of disobedience to God's command. Death would result from *sin*.

If that tree had not been in the garden, Adam and Eve would have obeyed and loved God because they had no other choice. But God wanted to fellowship with thinking beings who *chose* to love Him. So God placed that tree in the garden, giving them a choice.

Adam and Eve were allowed to eat freely from the Tree of Life. If they had ignored the forbidden tree, they would have lived forever. They would have filled the earth with their descendants, and the entire planet would have been a paradise.

But then the serpent appeared in the garden. Pleasing in appearance, he approached Eve: "Did God really say, 'You must not eat from all the trees of the garden'?"

Eve responded: "Of the fruit of the trees, we may eat. But of the fruit of the tree which is in the middle of the garden, God said, 'You must not eat of it and you must not touch it, or you will die.'"

Eve twisted the truth—God didn't say they couldn't *touch* the tree.

The serpent replied, "You most assuredly won't die! For God knows that when you eat of it, your eyes will be opened and you will be like God, knowing good and evil" (Genesis 3:1–5).

The serpent responded to Eve as she had answered him—with truth and with a twist. God *did* know that eating from the tree would open His children's eyes. But Adam and Eve would never be God, and if they sinned, they *would* die.

So through the serpent's tempting words and Eve and Adam's decisions, sin and death entered the world. And as Satan had predicted, their eyes were opened—to guilt, shame, and fear. To a host of emotions that tore at their hearts. Their Creator had lovingly designed them, given them everything they needed, including free will, and they had chosen to oppose the will of their Father.

Standing naked in the heavy silence, Adam and Eve staggered beneath the weight of their guilt. Flooded by remorse, terrified lest God see their sin, they took leaves from the lush vegetation and attempted to hide their shame.

As the evening breeze whispered through the garden, Adam and Eve heard the approach of their loving Father. Distressed because He would see what they had become, they hid themselves.

"Where are you?" God called.

Of course, He knew where they were, and from eternity past, God knew that love involves risk. He also knew what would happen after Adam and Eve sealed the fate of humanity. He had given them free will, and their disobedience had turned their desire to obey into an inclination to yield to their own desires. Their free will became a natural bent toward sin, and all their descendants would inherit that same tendency to sin.

God listened as Adam blamed Eve, and Eve blamed the serpent. Then the Lord cursed the serpent to crawl on his belly for the rest of his life. This was no ordinary snake; this was "the ancient serpent, called the devil and satan, who deceives the whole world" (Revelation 12:9).

Because God loved Adam and Eve, He would forgive them, and His forgiveness would be costly.

God said to the serpent, "I will put animosity between you and the woman—between your seed and her seed. He will crush your head, and you will crush his heel" (Genesis 3:15).

This verse has been called the *protevangelium*, the initial proclamation of the Gospel. It's the first of many prophecies that foretell Christ's birth, life, death, and resurrection. Satan would crush Christ's heel and cause much suffering, but Christ would crush the serpent's head.

With those words, God foretold that the Savior would come from the seed of the woman, not the man.[1] Isaiah 7:14 explained further: "Behold, the *virgin* will conceive." The oldest uncensored Jewish source texts make references to this miraculous birth, one of them stating that "the Messiah will be born from a 'closed womb.'"[2]

After promising deliverance from the effects of their sin, God made garments of animal skins to clothe Adam and Eve, rehabilitating their dignity by covering their shame. Innocent animals died to restore their fellowship with God, demonstrating that atonement for sin requires the shedding of innocent blood.

God expelled the first man and woman from Eden, so they no longer had access to the Tree of Life. Cherubim guarded the entrance (Genesis 3:24).

Scholars have tried to pinpoint the exact location of Eden, but it has been veiled from mortal eyes. I believe it now exists in a spiritual dimension, and those whose sins have been forgiven are allowed entry when their mortal bodies—which still hold a sin nature—perish. *Eden*, you see, is another word for *Paradise*, and Jesus told the thief on the cross, "I promise that you will be with me today in Gan-'Eden" (Luke 23:43 CJB).

Jesus—the innocent sacrifice for the sins of all people—provides entrance to the Garden of God, where redeemed human beings can enjoy the life God wanted for Adam and Eve. The apostle John wrote, "He who has an ear, let him hear what the *Ruach* [Spirit] is saying to Messiah's communities. To the one who overcomes, I will grant the right to eat from the Tree of Life, which is in the Paradise of God" (Revelation 2:7).

Christmas began in the garden because that's where sin entered the world and required a cure. Because we are Adam's descendants, we have inherited a fallen nature. "For since death came through a man," Paul wrote, "the resurrection of the dead also has come through a Man [Jesus]. For as in Adam all die, so also in Messiah will all be made alive" (1 Corinthians 15:21–22).

A Moment for Wonder

The most significant events in history occurred in Eden. God knew Adam and Eve would choose to sin and Jesus would have to redeem corrupted creation. God also knew the final result would be worth the suffering and sacrifice. In Paradise, He would finally be able to fellowship with people created in His image, people who had freely chosen Him and learned to love Him.

After turning Adam and Eve out of the garden, God waited. While He waited, He taught people through signs, patterns, and prophets. He called Abram to leave his home in southern Babylonia and established the nation of Israel through that obedient man.

He waited as the Israelites suffered in Egypt, and then He sent Moses to deliver them. He gave the children of Israel a Holy Law. He waited until they had completely disobeyed that Law and the warnings of His prophets, then sent them into a seventy-year-long Babylonian exile.

Yet He did not leave them hopeless. Through His prophets, He spoke of a coming Prophet and King, a righteous Branch who would shoot up like a sapling from the trunk of Jesse.

He waited until the civilized world was connected with roads, until His people lived again in Israel and longed desperately for their Messiah.

Then God sent His unique, divine Son.

The birth of Jesus Christ is the cornerstone of God's plan for the human race.

As you prepare for another Christmas, consider the scope of history—from the first until the last, everything in the divine plan revolves around the incarnation and birth of Christ.

Father, as we prepare for another Christmas season, help us to see the big picture—the beginning and the end, the human failure, and the future glorious finish. Make us mindful . . . and grateful.

3

THE SHEPHERD'S FIELD

Remember the old game of gossip or telephone? You whispered something in someone's ear, that individual whispered it to the next person in the circle, and so on. By the time your words made their way back to you, they no longer made sense!

For the last couple of years, I've received copies of an essay about newborn lambs raised by shepherds outside Bethlehem. The essay stated that shepherds in ancient Israel looked for perfect lambs that could be used for sacrifice. They would place newborn lambs in a stone manger to search for defects. If they found none, the lamb would be swaddled and kept in the manger to be protected. So, the essay said, when angels told the shepherds to look for a baby swaddled and lying in a manger, they knew immediately where to go and what they would find—the perfect Lamb of God, intended for sacrifice.

That's a lovely word picture, but it doesn't mesh with what we know about Bethlehem shepherds and their flocks. Nearly all the flocks around Bethlehem—sheep, cattle, and oxen—were intended for Temple sacrifice. The shepherds didn't have to search for "perfect" sacrificial candidates because unless an animal was sickly, scarred, or disfigured, it would qualify. Unblemished lambs were the rule, not the exception.

Newborn lambs must bond with their mothers within the first thirty minutes after birth, so no shepherd would ever separate a ewe from her offspring. As soon as a lamb is born, the mother licks it until it stands and begins to nurse. If mother and baby are kept apart, the ewe may abandon her offspring. Unless the lamb can bond with another ewe, it will die.

Why would anyone keep a newborn lamb in a manger? A swaddled lamb in a manger would not be able to walk or nurse. It would not survive more than a couple of days.

The Torah warns against separating a newborn from its mother for at least seven days (Exodus 22:29). And newborns were never sacrificed. The minimum age for a sacrifice was eight days[1] (Leviticus 22:27), and Passover lambs were one-year-old males "without defect" (Exodus 12:5). God required that sacrificial animals be "without blemish" because God requires something of real worth, not our second best.

One version of the "swaddled lamb" essay mentioned the tower of the flock, Migdal-eder, and a stone manger, presuming this was where the shepherds headed when the angels told them to look for a baby in a feeding trough.

The opposite is much more likely. The shepherds would have been encamped at Migdal-eder as they watched their flocks. From the height of the tower they could see all the animals in the fields. The tower was some distance away from

Bethlehem, so that was where they were when they heard the angel's announcement. After hearing the angel's news, the shepherds said, "Let's go to Bethlehem and see this thing . . ." (Luke 2:15).

Jesus was most likely born in Bethlehem, not in a field or a cave. The perfect Lamb of God was born, swaddled, and placed in a manger within the city walls.

Were lambs ever swaddled? I was astounded to learn they often were—but not immediately after birth. They weren't *completely* swaddled because they needed to be able to walk and nurse. But just as puppies and kittens are born with fuzzy fur, a lamb's birth-coat is especially soft, embellished with long, fine hairs that form a gentle "halo" around the lamb's body.

The practice of collecting this "halo hair" wool began as early as the fourth century before Christ and continues today. Talmudic sources tell us that to protect the wool of young lambs, shepherds kept Awassi sheep, the most common breed in Israel, in a protective cover from two to fifteen months of age. This wrapping averted the need for repeated washing and helped the halo-hair wool retain important lanolin.[2] These coverings were replaced as the lamb grew, and when the animal was old enough, the extra-soft wool was shorn and sold.

A Moment for Wonder

I shook my head when I first read the story of the swaddled lambs. I pictured a tiny, mummified lamb lying stiff-legged in a stone trough, unable to walk or nurse. Poor thing!

But the shepherds' actual historic practice of lamb-swaddling considers the lamb's need for nourishment, exercise, and emotional bonding with its mother. The covering is both protective and practical.

When we hold our first babies in our arms, we are often overprotective, too, determined not to allow any harmful influence near the child. But by the time we have gained a little experience, we realize that children need to be able to walk and run, enjoy new experiences, and learn from their mistakes.

How many times have we asked God to protect us from life's bumps and bruises? We ask for angels of protection to shield us from pain, and sometimes we ask amiss. In Gethsemane, Jesus prayed, "I am not asking that You take them out of the world, but that You keep them from the evil one" (John 17:15).

We do not need to be so protected that we lie helpless in a stone structure, unable to interact with the world. We need to be able to walk, talk, and engage with new acquaintances so we can share the truth of Christmas. We need to be protected from evil so we can courageously interact with those who don't know our Savior.

The world is what Jesus came to save. The world is filled with people our Father loves. We are to ask for protection from the evil one, but the world is our shepherds' field. Venture into it with joy and gladness, listening for the voice of your Father.

Father, we don't want to be mummified lambs. Don't let us retreat into the safety of our homes, our churches, or our neighborhoods, but give us eyes and ears for the people within and without our local areas. Help us to see people as you see them. Let us hear their unspoken cries. And protect us from the evil one as we venture out.

We offer this Christmas season to you. Show us how we can reach people outside our families and lead us to those who need to be reminded of the real reason for this holy season.

4

THE EASTERN KINGDOM

Thirteen hundred years before the birth of Christ, the Hebrews left Egypt and marched toward the Promised Land. Their approach terrified the kings in that region, so Balak, king of Moab, sent for a seer named Balaam. Balak offered Balaam great riches if he would curse the children of Israel.

Imagine Balaam's surprise when he muttered his incantations and heard, not from a demon, but from Almighty God. God told Balaam not to say a word apart from what He told him to say. After blessing Israel twice, Balaam again heard the voice of God and gave the frustrated king yet another blessing for Israel:

> "I see him, yet not at this moment.
> I behold him, yet not in this location.
> For a **star** will come from Jacob,
> a **scepter** will arise from Israel. . . ."
>
> Numbers 24:17 (emphasis added)

Balaam's prophecy was recorded in the Scriptures. When Babylon destroyed Jerusalem in 586 BC, copies of those

Scriptures were carried by captive Jews as they were marched to Babylon.

While in Babylon, devout Jews like Daniel, Shadrach, Meshach, and Abednego earned positions of authority in the king's court. Daniel, who remained faithful to his God, answered the king's questions when the royal wise men could not and even saved their lives (Daniel 2:24). In gratitude, Nebuchadnezzar made Daniel chief of the wise men.

Is it not possible that some of those wise men came to believe in Daniel's God?

As time passed, the wise men of the Medo-Persian kingdom probably read the Hebrew Scriptures as well as Daniel's book of prophecy. They and their successors would have been familiar with Balaam's prophecy about a star and a scepter rising from Israel. They would have read Daniel's prophecy of seventy weeks, which predicted "the time of *Mashiach the Prince*" to be 483[1] years after the issuing of a decree to restore and rebuild Jerusalem—a decree issued by Artaxerxes in 444 BC (Daniel 9:25–26).

Daniel was not the only righteous Jew the Persians would have known. They would subsequently become acquainted with Mordecai, Queen Esther, Nehemiah, and Ezra, a scribe, priest, and Torah teacher who led the exiles from Babylon back to Judea.

Wise men in the East counted the passing years and searched the sky. And though they had the Hebrew Scriptures that existed at the time of the exile, they did not have the book of Micah, a latter prophet, so they didn't know where the king would be born.

Now after *Yeshua* was born in Bethlehem of Judea, in the days of King Herod, magi from the east came to Jerusalem, saying, "Where is the One who has been born King of the Jews? For we saw His star in the east and have come to worship Him."

When King Herod heard, he was troubled, and all Jerusalem with him. And when he had called together all the ruling *kohanim* [priests] and *Torah* scholars, he began to inquire of them where the Messiah was to be born. So they told him, "In Bethlehem of Judea, for so it has been written by the prophet:

'And you, Bethlehem, land of Judah, are by no means least among the rulers of Judah;

For out of you shall come a ruler who will shepherd My people Israel'" [Micah 5:1]. . . .

After listening to the king, they went their way. And behold, the star they had seen in the east went on before them, until it came to rest over the place where the Child was. When they saw the star, they rejoiced exceedingly with great gladness. And when they came into the house, they saw the Child with His mother Miriam [*Mary*]; and they fell down and worshiped Him.

Matthew 2:1–6, 9–11

The star guided the magi, not the shepherds. God sent a heavenly sign to guide these wise men from the East.

Some scholars believe the Bethlehem star was a conjunction of the planets Jupiter and Saturn, an alignment that occurs about every nineteen years and occurred in 7 BC. I'm not sure a predictable conjunction of stars—especially one that occurred with such regularity—could persuade the magi to form a caravan and set out for Jerusalem. And consider this: after the wise men visited Herod, the star *moved* and led them directly to the house where the child was. It then disappeared after the wise men's departure, thwarting Herod's attempt to find and destroy the child.

I believe the Bethlehem star could have been the Shekinah, the visible glory of God.

You may not find the word *Shekinah* in your Bible translation; instead, you may read about "the glory of the Lord" or another visible manifestation of God's presence. The word comes from the word *shachan*, meaning "to dwell or abide."

Moses experienced the Shekinah when he spotted a bush that was on fire but not consumed by the flames. As he led the children of Israel out of Egypt, the Shekinah *moved* as a pillar of fire by night and a cloud by day. It moved purposefully, just like the Bethlehem star did many years later.

The Shekinah glory, reflected from God, left Moses' face with a residual glow as he came down from Mount Sinai. That same glory filled the Tabernacle when the Jews camped in the desert. That same glory filled the Temple when Solomon dedicated it, and then it moved into the Holy of Holies.

But when the people fell into sin, the Shekinah left the Temple, though in stages. First, the Shekinah moved from the Holy of Holies to the threshold of the Temple door and then to the Eastern Gate. Later, as the prophet Ezekiel had forewarned, the Shekinah rose and hovered over the Mount of Olives before vanishing altogether (Ezekiel 10:18–19; 11:22–23).

Years later, when Jesus was born, the Shekinah glory resided in a new abode—the physical body of Jesus Christ:

And the Word became flesh and tabernacled among us. We looked upon His glory, the glory of the one and only from the Father, full of grace and truth.

John 1:14

The shepherds didn't see the star, but they saw the Shekinah glory around the angels (Luke 2:9).

Peter, who witnessed the Transfiguration with James and John, later wrote: ". . . we saw his majesty with our own eyes. For we were there when he received honor and glory from God the Father; and the voice came to him from the grandeur of the *Sh'khinah*, saying, 'This is my son, whom I love; I am well pleased with him!'" (2 Peter 1:16–17 CJB).

Those who followed Yeshua during His ministry beheld His glory, though they did not always understand what they were witnessing. Isaiah prophesied of that day when he wrote, "The people walking in darkness will see a great light. Upon those dwelling in the land of the shadow of death, light will shine" (Isaiah 9:1).

Fifty days after Passover, the Shekinah appeared as individual tongues of flame when the Holy Spirit baptized the believers, who waited in the upper room for the Comforter, the Spirit of God.

The visible glory of God had returned, but not to Herod's Temple. After Pentecost, it was housed in flesh, tabernacled in believers who would live, act, and pray in the power of the Holy Spirit.

The Light of the World lived among people . . . and still does.

A Moment for Wonder

Jesus no longer lives on earth in bodily form, but His children do. The Holy Spirit dwells inside believers, and we shine with the glory of God when we act in ways that glorify Him.

"Let your light shine before men," Jesus said, "so they may see your good works and glorify your Father in heaven" (Matthew 5:16).

At Christmastime we delight in light. We pull jumbled cords from the attic and climb ladders to hang lights from the eaves of our porches. We bring Christmas trees into our homes and string them with lights so our homes will be warmed by their twinkling displays.

A legend credits Martin Luther for lighting the first Christmas tree with candles to show his children how beautiful the stars were when glimpsed from within the forest at nighttime. But perhaps the truest and best use of Christmas lights is to remind us of the Shekinah glory, the light that came to expel darkness from the human heart.

God is light, and in Him there is no darkness. Matthew, Mark, and Luke wrote of the end of the age when darkness would envelop the earth and terrify humankind (Matthew 24:29; Mark 13:24; Luke 21:25). But that dense darkness will disappear when Jesus returns with "power and great glory." The brightness of the Shekinah will illuminate the whole earth, demonstrating to everyone that Christ has come again!

Father, as we go about our work today, remove any sin or fault that would keep your glory from shining on those around us.

Remind us, as often as necessary, that our lives are yours, and all glory belongs to you. Let us be windows of pure glass so your glory can spill out and warm every soul we meet.

Let us be like the eastern wise men who followed your glory, and the disciples who witnessed it in myriad situations. Don't let us hide your light under a basket, but show us how to let it shine, especially during this Christmas season.

5

THE TEMPLE

The miracle of Messiah's arrival did not end with the baby's birth. Forty days later, Mary and Joseph slipped away from the Bethlehem house and began the six-mile walk to Jerusalem.

Eight days after Jesus' birth, after the couple had found a more suitable place to stay, the new parents held their son's naming ceremony. Joseph publicly proclaimed that the child would be called *Yeshua*, a name unknown in his or Mary's family, a name meaning *salvation*.

In obedience to the Law, the baby was circumcised according to the covenant God established with Abraham (Genesis 17:10–14). The surrounding nations waited until their sons reached puberty before circumcising them, but God's claim on a son of Abraham's life began in infancy. From babyhood, circumcision would mark Yeshua as one of God's chosen people.

Since giving birth to her son, Mary had kept to herself because she was ceremonially unclean. Until she made her purification offering, she would be forbidden to touch any consecrated item or worship in a synagogue or the Temple.

Mary and Joseph entered the city and walked through the bustling streets. Several mikvehs stood south of the Temple Mount, so she handed the baby to Joseph and entered one. After slipping out of her veil and tunic, she walked into the pool, knelt, and immersed herself in the running water.

Immersion in a mikveh was only part of the purification process. Mary still had to complete a sacrifice and a redemption ritual. Since all firstborns belonged to Adonai, her son would have to be redeemed with a payment of five shekels. Two turtledoves, the offering specified for a poor woman, would serve as Mary's sin and purification offerings.

Joseph purchased two doves in the outer courtyard, and then Mary entered the Court of the Women. She spotted a man directing new mothers to the steps that led from the Court of the Women to the Court of Isra'el. As the worshipers' prayers rose and the attending priests entered the space with the golden altar, she must have thanked God for bringing her through the rigors and risks of childbirth.

Jewish women were not blind to the scriptural significance of childbearing. "Each time a woman gives birth," they often said, "she approaches death. Through great travail, she strikes the serpent who tempted Eve. The serpent longs for our death, but when we bring forth life, we are victorious, even if we die."[1]

Mary approached the Gate of Nicanor and handed the wooden birdcage to a waiting Levite. The first bird paid for Mary's sins; the second was an offering for her purification.

Afterward, Mary found Joseph in the crowd, and together they went to another Levite for the redemption of the firstborn.

"'He who has sanctified us with His commandments and has commanded us to redeem the firstborn son,'" the Levite recited.

Joseph gave the proper response: "He who has given us life."

The priest put out his hand, and Joseph placed five silver shekels in the man's palm. "Your son is redeemed," the priest said, concluding the ceremony.

Joseph had no sooner turned from the priest when Simeon, a righteous *tzaddik*, shouted from across the court and strode toward them with an urgency that belied his years.

Neither Mary nor Joseph knew that God had made Simeon a promise: "And it had been revealed to him by the *Ruach ha-Kodesh* that he would not die before he had seen the Anointed One of ADONAI" (Luke 2:26).

The aging tzaddik took one look at the child in Mary's arms and extended his arms. A wavering smile shone through the man's long beard as Mary surrendered the baby.

"Now may You let Your servant go in peace, O Sovereign Master, according to Your word," Simeon said. "For my eyes have seen Your salvation, which You have prepared in the presence of all peoples: 'A light for revelation to the nations' [Gentiles] and the glory of Your people Israel" (Luke 2:29–32).

Simeon referenced a Messianic prophecy in Isaiah 49:6: "It is too trifling a thing that You should be My servant to raise up the tribes of Jacob and restore the preserved ones of Israel. So I will give You as a light for the nations, that You should be My salvation to the end of the earth."

In only a few words, Simeon had declared two important truths. First, the Messiah would be a *light* for *revelation to the Gentiles*. A startling statement because at that point most Jews were not sure God wanted to do *anything* for the Gentiles. God had declared that Israel was His son, His firstborn (Exodus 4:22). The question of whether Gentiles could receive salvation had been debated by Jewish sages for generations, but Simeon proclaimed that Jesus had been born to bring salvation to *all*.

Simeon also said the Messiah would bring glory upon Israel. Jesus would be more than revelation to them; He would be the Shekinah Isaiah had predicted:

> Arise, shine, for your light has come!
> The glory of ADONAI has risen on you.
> For behold, darkness covers the earth,
> and deep darkness the peoples.
> But ADONAI will arise upon you,
> and His glory will appear over you.
> Nations will come to your light,
> kings to the brilliance of your rising.
>
> Isaiah 60:1–3

Then Simeon said to Mary, "Behold, this One is destined to cause the fall and rise of many in Israel, and to be a sign that is opposed, so the thoughts of many hearts may be uncovered. And even for you, a sword will pierce through your soul" (Luke 2:34–35).

Simeon foretold that Jesus would cause division in Israel. Those who received salvation would rise, and those who rejected salvation would fall. Jesus would be a "rock of offense" for many (Romans 9:33). And because He had been born to Mary, Jesus would cause a sword to pierce her soul.

"She was present when the Jewish leaders rejected Him and called Him demon-possessed," wrote Arnold Fruchtenbaum. "She observed the people turning against Him. The sword pierced its deepest when she saw her Son hanging upon the cross. . . . [Mary] herself will have to make up her mind about the salvation her Son offers, as her child is set for the falling and the rising of many in Israel, including her."[2]

Before Joseph and Mary left the Temple, an elderly woman, Anna, approached them. Mary might have recognized her as a prophetess who for years had been a fixture in the Court of Women. A widow, Anna did nothing but pray and worship day and night, fasting and pleading with Adonai for the salvation of Isra'el.

Luke doesn't tell us exactly what Anna said, except that "she began praising God and speaking about the Child to all those waiting for the redemption of Jerusalem" (Luke 2:38).

The others in the Temple must have been filled with joy . . . or perhaps bewilderment. Could this unassuming couple's infant possibly be Israel's long-awaited Messiah?

A Moment for Wonder

We think of the Christmas story as joyful, and rightly so. But just as a tapestry is woven of bright *and* dark threads, the joy of the Nativity must be juxtaposed against the suffering of the sacrifice. Simeon's words to Mary and Joseph were filled with hope, joy, and pain.

As human beings, we are averse to suffering. No one enjoys going to the dentist, and no one volunteers to experience pain unless motivated by some degree of love. A mother would donate a kidney to save her child's life. A firefighter would rush into a burning building to rescue someone who's trapped. Parents will skip lunch to buy Christmas gifts for their kids, and people will donate to give the less fortunate a delicious turkey dinner.

For love, most of us are willing to set aside our comfort if we can help someone else. Magnify that impulse by infinity and you can *almost* understand the love that compelled God the Father to send His Son, and the Son's willingness to endure the pain, weakness, and humility of being born in human flesh. Of becoming a rock of offense and a stone of stumbling. Of being spurned by His own family.

Is there some task or meeting you've been dreading this month? Perhaps you need to have a difficult conversation with someone. Perhaps you need to steel yourself against the pain and say what needs to be said . . . with love.

Perhaps you need to risk discomfort to reach out to someone who needs you. Know this: you could never love that person as much as God does.

Father, we acknowledge that we have been called to experience your suffering as well as your joy. You never said the Christian life would be easy, but you promised that your Spirit would comfort, guide, and keep us always. Help us to be like Mary, who pondered Anna's and Simeon's words and kept them in her heart, knowing that her future suffering would pale in comparison to the ultimate victory.

6

EGYPT

We couldn't tell the complete story of Jesus' birth without mentioning Egypt. Though the children of Israel were once enslaved by that nation, God used Egypt to save the Jews on three separate occasions.

Known as the "Black Land" on account of its flood-enriched soil, Egypt was famous for its fertility and wealth. Genesis 12:10 contains the first biblical mention of this ancient kingdom: "Now there was a famine in the land. So Abram went down to Egypt to live as an outsider there. . . ."

The people of Canaan, where Abram was dwelling, were starving because the rains had not come. To save his family, slaves, and livestock, Abram and his household traveled to Egypt knowing they would be outsiders. Yet starvation posed a greater danger, so Abram risked everything and immigrated to the Black Land.

On the way, he had a word with Sarai, his wife: "Look, please, I know that you are an attractive woman. So when the Egyptians see you they'll say, 'This is his wife.' And they'll kill me; but you, they'll let live. Please say that you are my sister, so that I'll be treated well for your sake, and my life will be spared because of you" (Genesis 12:11–13).

Just as Abram feared, the men of Egypt *did* notice Sarai, and they raved about her beauty to Pharaoh. Sarai was taken to the king's house, apparently to prepare for a royal marriage. Because Pharaoh believed Abram was her brother, the king gave him sheep, cattle, donkeys, slaves, and camels.

Because God was not pleased that Pharaoh had taken Sarai, He struck the king's household with plagues. Somehow Pharaoh learned the reason and confronted Abram: "Why didn't you tell me that she is your wife? Why did you say, 'She is my sister,' so that I took her to be my wife? Now, here is your wife. Take—and go!" (Genesis 12:18–19).

The Egyptians sent Abram and Sarai away, and they left the land with far more wealth than they had brought into Egypt. But they—and their unborn descendants—survived the famine.

Fast-forward three generations. Joseph, son of Jacob and great-grandson of Abram, has prophetic dreams about his brothers and parents bowing down to him. These dreams irk his family, and his ten jealous half brothers decide to rid themselves of the spoiled favorite. They soak his coat in blood and set it aside to show to their father as evidence of Joseph's "accidental death." Then they sell their brother to a group of traders who are heading to Egypt.

You probably know the story: Joseph is sold into slavery, where he serves a man named Potiphar, until Potiphar's wife decides to seduce the handsome young slave. Joseph flees temptation, but Potiphar cannot honor his slave above his wife. As a result, Joseph is thrown in prison, where he remains until Pharaoh has a troubling nightmare. A former prisoner remembers that Joseph has a gift for interpreting dreams, so Joseph is brought out of prison, then shaved, scrubbed, and presented to the powerful ruler.

Relying upon guidance from God, Joseph correctly interprets the king's dream and becomes Pharaoh's vizier—the second most powerful position in Egypt. He is now thirty years old, with thirteen years spent in the Black Land. He has been given a new Egyptian name and an Egyptian wife.

The next seven years produce a bountiful harvest; the following seven bring a severe famine. Word of the Egyptian bounty travels quickly, and caravans throughout the land set out for Egypt, where Joseph holds the keys to the royal granaries. Knowing that famine had struck the entire world, Joseph tells his men to watch for a group of brothers from Canaan.

When ten of Joseph's eleven brothers arrive, Joseph looks Egyptian, dresses like an Egyptian, and speaks Egyptian. The brothers are his family, but they don't recognize him.

To test their hearts, Joseph accuses them of being spies. The brothers insist they are the innocent sons of one man.

Joseph holds one of them hostage—Simeon, the brother with the quickest temper—and gives the others food. He sends them home and says if they return, they must bring their youngest brother.

As the brothers travel home, they probably beg God to end the famine so they will never have to encounter the vizier again.

Instead, the grain runs out before the rains return. Despite their elderly father's heartrending protests, they take their youngest brother, Benjamin, to Egypt. They stand before the king's vizier, who abruptly excuses himself because he's moved to tears by the sight of his precious younger brother.

Joseph instructs a servant to take a valuable silver divining bowl and hide it in Benjamin's bag. Simeon is returned to them, the brothers are given more grain, and again they leave for home. But Joseph's guards catch up with the traveling party and accuse the brothers of stealing Joseph's property. The brothers deny everything—that is, until the bowl is found in Benjamin's bag.

The brothers are escorted to Joseph's palace, where Judah begs to remain behind as a slave so Benjamin can return to his loving father.

Faced with this evidence of their changed hearts, Joseph orders the servants out of the room, then reveals himself to his brothers. He asks about his father, and when his brothers are too terrified to respond, he tells them not to fear. "God sent me ahead of you," he explains, "to ensure a remnant in the land and to keep you alive for a great escape. So now, it wasn't you, you didn't send me here, but God!" (Genesis 45:7–8).

God sent Joseph to Egypt to save Israel from the famine. Joseph suffered many things—loneliness, treachery, imprisonment and its violence—yet he was elevated in God's timing. One day his people will look to him and wonder about the Messiah. More on that later.

"Although Joseph is not personally mentioned in the New Testament as a type of Christ," Alfred Edersheim wrote, "his history was eminently typical of that of our blessed Savior, alike in his betrayal, his elevation to highest dignity, and his preserving the life of his people, and in their ultimate recognition of him and repentance of their sin. Yet, though 'known to God' were all these . . . works from the beginning, all parties were allowed, in the free exercise of their own choice, to follow their course, ignorant that all the while they were only contributing their share towards the fulfilment of God's purposes."[1]

As I mentioned, the Christmas story would not be complete without considering the third time God saved Israel through Egypt. After the magi left Mary, Joseph, and young Jesus in Bethlehem, an angel warned Joseph in a dream: "Get up! Take the Child and His mother and flee to Egypt. Stay there until I tell you, for Herod is about to search for the Child, to kill Him" (Matthew 2:13).

Joseph rose, and that very night he took Jesus and Mary and left for Egypt. "This," Matthew wrote, "was to fulfill what was spoken by ADONAI through the prophet, saying, 'Out of Egypt I called My son'" (2:15; Hosea 11:1).

But this time the migrating Jewish family wouldn't be outsiders. Jews had been moving to Egypt since the time of the Babylonian exile, with many settling in Alexandria. Since the arrival of the Greek general who took control after Alexander the Great's death, the land of Egypt had been thoroughly Hellenized. The succeeding pharaohs, including Cleopatra, were not Egyptians, but Greeks.

We do not know how long Jesus and His family lived in Egypt, but we know He and His parents were probably surrounded by

Jews who worshiped in synagogues and supported the young family. Even in this, God had prepared the land and the people for the One who was to come.

A Moment for Wonder

If you have Jewish friends or family who have not met Jesus, be sensitive to them at Christmastime. Seth Postell, Eitan Bar, and Erez Soref explain why: "Our people will not understand who Yeshua is in the context of Christmas trees. . . . They do, however, value Sabbath rest, Passover redemption, the solemnity of the Day of Atonement, and the beauty of kindled lights. In this context, Yeshua no longer appears like Joseph disguised as an Egyptian, but as Joseph, revealed as our brother!"[2]

You are already learning about the Jewish roots of our faith. Continue to learn and share the prophecies of the Messiah with your Jewish friends, gently revealing the truth about who Yeshua was—the only descendant of David who fulfilled the Old Testament prophecies of the Messiah's lineage and birthplace.

Father, help us to be respectful and loving toward Yeshua's people, the Jews. We acknowledge that we owe them a great debt, and it is only through your love and mercy that we have been grafted onto their tree. Use us as you will and give us wisdom as we humbly share what we have learned about the Messiah, who came to save Jews and Gentiles alike.

As Isaiah wrote, "Also the foreigners who join themselves to Adonai, to minister to Him, and to love the Name of Adonai, and to be His servants . . . these I will bring to My holy mountain . . . For My House will be called a House of Prayer for all nations" (Isaiah 56:6–7).

7

NAZARETH

And he [Joseph] went and lived in a city called Natzeret, to fulfill what was spoken through the prophets, that Yeshua shall be called a Natzrati.

Matthew 2:23

There are two opinions about what Matthew meant when he wrote this verse. The first is that the word *Natzrati* should be translated *Nazoraios*, which is akin to the Hebrew participle *nat-zur*, meaning "one who is protected or kept." Those who interpret the verse this way believe Matthew was referring to Hosea 11:1, saying that Jesus was called out of Egypt where He had been protected, just as Israel was protected in a time of famine.[1]

Nothing in Scripture contradicts that interpretation, but the prevailing opinion holds that Matthew was in fact referring to Isaiah 11:1:

Then a shoot will come forth out of the stem of Jesse,
and a branch will bear fruit out of His roots.

Matthew may have been employing a play on words: *Nazareth* comes from the Hebrew word *netzer*, which means *branch* or *off-shoot*. Matthew 2:23 correctly confirms Isaiah's prophecy that the Messiah would come from the line of Jesse, father to King David.

Nestled against a hillside, Nazareth was situated halfway between the Mediterranean and the Sea of Galilee. At the time, Nazareth was a town of less than five hundred people, not as small as Bethlehem or as large as Jerusalem. A major highway, the Via Maris, cut through it, so the people of Nazareth were accustomed to seeing travelers from far-flung nations at the village well.

The people of Nazareth were also accustomed to seeing Romans because the city housed the Roman garrison that controlled northern Galilee. Jewish hatred of the Romans was so intense that some suspected the city's residents of "consorting with the enemy." To call someone a *Nazarene* indicated utter contempt.[2]

When Philip told his brother Nathanael that he had found the one Moses and the prophets wrote about, Nathanael replied, "Natzeret! Can anything good come from there?" (John 1:46).

But something—Someone—did, the Branch of David, the Servant Messiah.

Like most Jewish towns, Nazareth had at least one place of worship. During Israel's time of exile, any settlement with at least ten Jewish men (a *minyan*) could establish a synagogue. In a typical service, the leader would open with prayer, then Torah teachers would read from the Scriptures and expound on the reading.

Not long after beginning His earthly ministry, Jesus returned to His hometown and attended the synagogue on Shabbat. He would have seen familiar faces, recognizing people He had known all his life. These people knew His parents, His half-siblings, His nephews and nieces. Some of them may have hired Joseph, Jesus, or one of his brothers for a building project.

He would have walked into the synagogue's southern entrance with the other worshipers, filing past the *Tevah*, the Ark containing the sacred scrolls of the Torah and the prophets. Because He had begun to teach and preach, He must have been invited to read part of the Scriptures at the Shabbat service. One always stood to read Scripture and sat to teach.

When the scroll of the prophet Isaiah was handed to Him, Jesus stood, opened the scroll, and found the place where it was written,

> "The Ruach ADONAI is on me,
> because He has anointed me
> to proclaim Good News to the poor.
> He has sent me to proclaim release to the captives
> and recovery of sight to the blind,
> to set free the oppressed,
> and to proclaim the year of ADONAI's favor."
>
> He closed the scroll, gave it back to the attendant, and sat down. All eyes in the synagogue were focused on Him.
>
> Luke 4:18–20

Why was every eye focused on Jesus? Because He had violated rabbinic tradition by only reading half the required number of verses. What was He thinking?

In hindsight, His actions made sense. He could not read the entire prophecy (vv. 1–3) because the remaining verses were not being fulfilled that day.[3]

Jesus looked at His neighbors and said, "Today this Scripture has been fulfilled in your ears" (Luke 4:21). His listeners must have blinked in confusion. Was this a prelude to some extraordinary miracle, or something else? They had heard about His miracles in Capernaum and wanted to see something amazing with their own eyes.

Jesus continued: "Doubtless you will say to Me this proverb, 'Doctor, heal yourself!' and 'What we have heard was done at Capernaum, do as much here also in your hometown.'

"Truly, I tell you, 'No prophet is accepted in his own hometown.' But with all truthfulness I say to you, that there were many widows in Israel in the days of Elijah, when heaven was closed for three and a half years and there came a great famine over all the land. Elijah was not sent to any of them, but only to Zarephath in the land of Sidon, to a widowed woman. There were many with *tzara'at* [leprosy] in Israel in the time of Elisha the prophet, and none of them were purified apart from Naaman the Syrian" (Luke 4:23–27).

Imagine the silence that followed. Was He implying that Capernaum's people had more faith than those of Nazareth? And why was He talking about *Gentiles*? Why wasn't He presenting His bona fides, giving them the inside story of His mission? And why had He implied that they didn't understand when *they* knew Him like no one else?

That was the problem. They knew Him as the carpenter's son. They were willing to accept Him as a revolutionary, even a prophet, but they were not willing to see Him as the long-awaited Branch, the Messiah and Son of God. The very idea infuriated them:

> Now all in the synagogue were filled with rage upon hearing these things. Rising up, they drove Him out of the town and brought Him as far as the edge of the mountain on which their city had been built, in order to throw Him off the cliff. But passing through the middle of them, He went on His way.
>
> Luke 4:28–30

As far as we know, the people of Nazareth knew next to nothing about who Jesus *really* was. They wanted a healer and a freedom fighter, not a teacher who talked about Gentiles and worked miracles in Capernaum.

Why didn't God open their eyes? Did He want them to remain in the dark? Perhaps for a while, at least. Because others needed saving, too. Consider Isaiah 53:3, translated from the Hebrew:

> He is despised, and left of men,
> A man of pains, and acquainted with sickness,
> And as one hiding the face from us,
> He is despised, and we esteemed him not (YLT).

Could God have intended to hide the Messiah from the majority of His chosen people?

The passage from Isaiah implies that the Messiah would be like "one hiding the face" from His people. Did God ever hide other deliverers?

Remember Joseph? Though He suffered imprisonment and slavery, after many years he was elevated to a throne and reunited with his family.

Though Jesus suffered imprisonment and death, He has been elevated and will one day be recognized and worshiped by His Jewish family (Zechariah 12:10).

Joseph's brothers did not recognize him because they saw him exalted on a throne.

Jesus' neighbors did not recognize Him because they saw Him as the carpenter's son.

While Joseph was hidden from his brothers, he saved thousands who were not sons of Abraham.

While Jesus remains hidden from *most* Jews, He is saving thousands who are not sons of Abraham.

Yet the true nature of Jesus was not hidden from everyone in Nazareth. After His resurrection, His brothers and sisters accepted Him. They, and many others, recognized the Light of the World.

A Moment for Wonder

We of the twenty-first century have been exposed to so much *light*. We have access to Bibles, churches, television ministries, radio programs, Christian websites, and books galore. Surrounded by such illumination, it's sobering to realize so many still walk in darkness.

I was raised in a Christian family, so I made the decision to follow Christ as a child. But my husband and many of my friends surrendered their lives to Christ as adults, and they remember what their lives were like in the Before Christ days. Every party came with a hangover, every high came with a low. Relationships came and went, emotions vacillated wildly, and life often seemed pointless.

Perhaps you remember your own BC days. Let those memories soften your heart toward those who haven't yet met the Messiah. In our Bibles we have the necessary revelation of God—all we need to understand why and how Christ came—and we can share that good news. What better time to share it than during the month of December when half the world is celebrating Christmas? Take a string of lights to your agnostic friend and say, "Let me tell you about the *true* light born in Bethlehem . . ."

Father, as we go through this holiday season, open our eyes to notice opportunities to worship you by focusing on others. Remind us of our neighbors. How can we serve them? How can we demonstrate your love? How can we shine your light into their homes?

Don't let us be like the people of Nazareth. Instead, open our eyes, minds, and hearts to what Jesus said. And when we meet Jewish people, help us to show them love, respect, and honor because it's through Christ that we've been adopted into the family of Abraham. We worship you, Father God, and give you all praise and glory as we pray for the salvation of Israel.

FAMILY ACTIVITY FOR THE ADVENT SEASON

The Places: What If Jesus Were Born Today?

Most families are familiar with places associated with the birth of Jesus: the manger, the shepherds' field, and Jerusalem, home of the Temple. It might be fun for you and your children to talk about which places would be associated with Jesus were He born today in your part of the world.

If Mary and Joseph were traveling from your town to register for taxes, what would be their destination? If they could not find a hotel room, where would they sleep? An Airbnb? At a bus station? In a car?

And if they were traveling and Mary was ready to give birth, how would she cope if she had no insurance? What if there was no nearby hospital? She might end up having the baby on someone's air mattress, with a volunteer midwife to assist. Or an EMT. Or . . . who?

Instead of shepherds, who would the angel send to welcome the promised Messiah? Instead of wise men from the East, who might come from afar, and how would they travel to see the baby?

Finally, where would a modern Mary and Joseph go to record the baby's birth? Who would be in the building, and who might recognize the baby as the long-promised hope for the world?

Read through the second chapter of Luke with your family and substitute modern places and people for the historical names. This exercise may seem ludicrous, but it could help children realize just how frightening Mary and Joseph's situation would have been, and how miraculous God's arrangements were for them.

In closing, lead your family in prayer and thank God for having prepared the places and people Mary and Joseph encountered on their journeys to Bethlehem, Egypt, and Nazareth. God planned everything even before Eden, and His prophets foretold an amazing number of details.

PART 2

THE PROPHECIES
OF CHRISTMAS

8

PROPHECIES OF THE COMING MESSIAH

At the time of Jesus' birth, the Jews' longing for Messiah's arrival had never been stronger.

Since 63 BC, Judea had been one of Rome's client kingdoms. The Romans installed Herod the Great as king, and he reigned until 4 BC. After Herod's death, his sons ruled different areas of Judea, but Rome maintained control.

The Romans, who were polytheists and quite willing to accommodate the religious beliefs of other cultures, did not know what to make of the monotheistic Jews. They expected the Jews to politely acknowledge the Roman gods and were offended when the Jews refused to do so.

The Jews, on the other hand, resented Rome's military occupation, taxation, and its meddling with the office of high priest. The Romans even retained custody of the high priest's sacred garments except for when needed for annual rituals. Though the Romans didn't require the Jews to worship Caesar, they did require the people to offer prayers and sacrifices for the emperor.

The friction between Romans and Jews did not dissipate as time passed. In fact, the situation grew more tense with each passing year. While the Jews groaned under Roman occupation, their Torah teachers searched the Scriptures for hope. In Jesus' day, Lois Tverberg says, "Evidence suggests that the Torah was being read as if Israel's prophets were its commentators, elaborating on how each detail of the Torah would find fulfillment in the world to come."[1]

The sages weren't blind to the words of the prophets. They studied Isaiah 53 and Psalm 22:1–22 and realized the words were Messianic. But since they could not make sense of a suffering king, they declared that God would send *two* messiahs: a conquering King, Messiah, son of David; and a suffering servant, Messiah, son of Joseph. They reasoned that the suffering servant would spring from Joseph the patriarch because he had suffered mightily before God elevated him in Egypt.[2]

In the early days of Jesus' ministry, Philip told Nathanael, "We've found the One that Moses in the Torah, and also the prophets, wrote about—Yeshua of Natzeret, the son of Joseph!" (John 1:45). We know Philip was referring to Joseph the patriarch because the prophets did not write about Joseph the carpenter.

What the Jews did not expect was one Messiah and two appearances—the first as a helpless baby who arrived through a virgin's womb and came to suffer and die, the second (and still future) as conquering king who would descend through the clouds to reign over His creation. Even Jesus' disciples did not clearly understand His mission until after the resurrection (Acts 1:6).

When we examine the Scriptures first-century Jews considered Messianic, it's easy to see why they expected a warlike king.

We've already discussed the first prophecy, issued after Adam and Eve's sin: "I will put animosity between you and the woman—between your seed and her seed. He will crush your head, and you will crush his heel" (Genesis 3:15). A Messiah who "crushes" could easily be a warrior.

As Jacob lay on his deathbed, he sent for each of his twelve sons and blessed them. He blessed Judah, his fourth-born, with these words: "The scepter will not pass from Judah, nor the ruler's staff from between his feet, until he to whom it belongs will come. To him will be the obedience of the peoples" (Genesis 49:10). He spoke of a scepter, describing a king.

Another kingly prophecy came from Balaam: "I see him, yet not at this moment. I behold him, yet not in this location. For a star will come from Jacob, a scepter will arise from Israel" (Numbers 24:17).

A warrior-king Messiah would form an army and march against Rome to deliver His people from subjugation. As Jesus healed the sick and raised the dead, people pointed to the miracles as proof of His authority to rule. What a king He would be! When soldiers were wounded in battle, Jesus could heal them, even bring them back to life. If they hungered, He could miraculously supply food. If the environment worked against Jewish forces, Jesus could change the weather with a word.

This is one reason why so many Jews of Jesus' day did not recognize Him. The suffering man on the cross wasn't the Messiah they were expecting . . . or even the one they wanted.

A Moment for Wonder

With the blessing of hindsight and the leading of the Holy Spirit, we now realize that the Old Testament is replete with specific prophecies about the child born at Christmas.

The Messiah would come as a baby:

> For to us a child is born,
> a son will be given to us,
> and the government will be upon His shoulder.
> His Name will be called
> Wonderful Counselor,
> Mighty God
> My Father of Eternity,
> Prince of Peace.

Isaiah 9:5

The Messiah would be humble:

> Rejoice greatly, daughter of Zion!
> Shout, daughter of Jerusalem!
> Behold, your king is coming to you,
> a righteous one bringing salvation.
> He is lowly, riding on a donkey—
> on a colt, the foal of a donkey.

Zechariah 9:9

The Messiah would be a suffering servant:

> Behold, My servant will prosper,
> He will be high and lifted up and greatly exalted.
> Just as many were appalled at You—
> His appearance was disfigured more than any man,

His form more than the sons of men.
So He will sprinkle many nations.
Kings will shut their mouths because of Him,
for what had not been told them they will see,
and what they had not heard they will perceive.

Isaiah 52:13–15

The Messiah, an immortal being, would be born in Bethlehem:

But you, Bethlehem Ephrathah—
least among the clans of Judah—
from you will come out to Me
One to be ruler in Israel,
One whose goings forth are from of old,
from days of eternity.

Micah 5:1

The Messiah would be our salvation:

The Righteous One, My Servant will make many righteous
and He will bear their iniquities.
Therefore I will give Him a portion with the great,
and He will divide the spoil with the mighty—
because He poured out His soul to death,
and was counted with transgressors.
For He bore the sin of many,
and interceded for the transgressors.

Isaiah 53:11–12

Father, help us look in Scripture and see what is, not simply what we want to see. Open our minds and hearts to your truths and teach us your Word. We trust your Word, just as we trust you—our salvation, our Lord, and our God.

9

PROPHECIES IN PATTERNS

On some occasions a prophecy may seem to refer to two separate situations:

> When Israel was a youth I loved him, and out of Egypt I called My son.
>
> Hosea 11:1

Hosea wrote that verse while thinking of how God drew the children of Abraham out of Egyptian bondage. Yet Matthew quotes the prophet Hosea when he references Jesus and His parents coming out of Egypt after Herod's death. One Scripture, two meanings, both inspired by the Holy Spirit.

Some theologians refer to this dual meaning as the "law of double reference," but I like to think of it as a pattern: what happened once has happened again.

Consider Noah, a man who built an ark (*tevah*) and delivered his family from God's judgment during the flood.

Consider Moses, a child saved by an ark (*tevah*) who delivered his extended family from God's judgment in Egypt.

The rabbis have a saying: *"Ma'asei avot, simian l'banim,"* meaning *"The deeds of the fathers are a sign to the sons."* The stories recorded in Scripture speak not only about what has happened but also what will happen in the future.

Consider this passage where God speaks to David through Nathan the prophet:

> "It will be that when your days are fulfilled to go with your fathers, I will raise up your offspring after you, one of your own sons, and I will establish his kingdom. He will build a house for Me and I will establish his throne forever. I will be a father to him and he will be a son to Me, I will not withdraw My lovingkindness from him, as I withdrew it from the one who ruled before you. I will appoint him over My House and My kingdom forever, and his throne will be established forever."
>
> 1 Chronicles 17:11–14

This prophecy was partially fulfilled in Solomon. Under his leadership, the kingdom of Israel rose to its zenith, and he built the Temple, a house for God. But Solomon's foreign wives drew him away from God, and Israel divided after his death.

The *complete* fulfillment of the prophecy came through Jesus. He also built a house for God, the Church, and His throne has been established forever. God is His Father, and He will never withdraw His love.

Because the Old Testament mindset was more about illustrating than explaining, God used signs, patterns, and types to demonstrate what He was doing and what He had planned. For instance, the seventh chapter of Isaiah tells of two cooperating kings—Rezin of Aram and Pekah of Israel—who had attacked Jerusalem (see 2 Kings 15:37–16:9). When Ahaz, king of Judah, heard the enemy kings were determined to depose him, he was terrified. Despite Isaiah's assurance that God would not allow the city to be destroyed, Ahaz worried that he would die and the royal line of David would be wiped out.

So God sent Isaiah to the king and told the prophet to take along his young son, Shear-jashub. Isaiah told the king, "Ask for a sign from ADONAI your God—from the depths of Sheol or the heights of Heaven" (Isaiah 7:11).

Ahaz claimed false piety: "I won't ask—I wouldn't test ADONAI!" (7:12).

Isaiah must have sighed when he responded,

"Hear now, house of David! Is it a small thing for *you* [plural] to weary men? Will you also weary my God? Therefore ADONAI Himself will give you a sign:

> Behold, the virgin will conceive.
> When she is giving birth to a son,
> she will call his name Immanuel.
> He will be eating curds and honey
> by the time he knows to refuse evil and choose good.

For before the boy knows to refuse evil and choose good, the land of the two kings *you* [singular] dread will be abandoned."

Isaiah 7:13–16

In verse 13, Isaiah uses the Hebrew plural "you" to indicate that he is speaking to the entire house of David. The sign for David's house is that the virgin will give birth to a child who will be called "Immanuel" or "God with us." This miraculous child *will* come, and David's line will not be destroyed.

Then Isaiah uses the Hebrew singular *you* because he addresses Ahaz alone. Perhaps he gestured to the young boy in his arms. "Before the boy knows the difference between right and wrong," he told Ahaz, "the threat against you will be removed."[1]

The prophecy came to pass just as Isaiah had predicted. Before Isaiah's son reached an age of accountability, the enemy kings had ceased to exist.[2]

Here's another pattern: when God placed Adam in the garden, Adam was king of creation and a priest who talked directly with God. God blessed him and gave him dominion over the earth. Adam was a priest and king, but he lost both positions when he sinned.

Then came Jesus, the One who would crush the serpent's head. He was the fulfillment of Messianic prophecies about a coming Priest and King, the second Adam. God blessed Him and will give Him dominion over all the earth (Daniel 7:14).

In Numbers 21, we read about venomous serpents who bit the complaining children of Israel. God gave Moses a cure: "Make yourself a fiery snake and put it on a pole. Whenever anyone who has been bitten will look at it, he will live" (v. 8).

Generations later, Jesus would tell Nicodemus, "Just as Moses lifted up the serpent in the desert, so the Son of Man must be lifted up, so that whoever believes in Him may have eternal life!" (John 3:14–15).

A Moment for Wonder

Adam's sin brought death to all people. The Messiah's death and resurrection brings life to all people who look to Him with *saving faith*. What is saving faith?

We have a president in the United States. I've seen videos of him. I *believe* he exists. This factual belief would be translated *noticia* in Greek. Depending on when you're reading this, I might have *believed* in our president enough to vote for him. I might have had *assensus* (Greek for *agreement*) with him.

But if I were taken prisoner tomorrow, do I *believe* our president would save me? Am I willing to trust him with my life? Do I have *fiducia* (Greek for *complete trust*) in the president?

Um . . . no. Our president is not all-powerful. He is not all-knowing. And he doesn't know me.

The English word *believe* can have three completely different meanings.

I *know* Jesus lived and died and rose again. I've read the historical evidence.

I *agree* with Him—I am a sinner and I need the salvation He provides.

Finally, I *trust* Him with my life. He not only knows me, He *loves* me.

A pattern of faith exists throughout Scripture, and without faith, it is impossible to please God (Hebrews 11:6).

Adam and Eve could not obey one simple command from God. The Israelites could not obey the 613 commands of the Law. The rules were about teaching people how to live, but salvation is and always has been about faith. Striving for holiness in our own strength always fails.

When God called Noah to build a boat, Noah *believed* and obeyed. I imagine his only question was "How big?"

When God called Abram to leave his country, Abram *believed*, packed his camels, and headed toward a foreign land. "Then he *believed* in ADONAI and He reckoned it to him as righteousness" (Genesis 15:6).

When God judged Egypt and spared the Hebrews, the children of Israel *believed*. "When Israel saw the great work that ADONAI did over the Egyptians, the people feared ADONAI, and they *believed* in ADONAI and in His servant Moses" (Exodus 14:31).

When God sent Jonah to preach to the Gentiles of Nineveh, they *believed* and were saved from destruction: "Then the people of Nineveh *believed* God and called for a fast and wore sackcloth—from the greatest of them to the least of them" (Jonah 3:5).

"For God so loved the world that He gave His one and only Son, that whoever *believes* in Him shall not perish but have eternal life" (John 3:16).

Loving God is not about rule-keeping. It's about believing in the Christmas child with your mind and emotions and entrusting your life to Him.

Father, it's so easy to get caught up in activities, shopping, and decorating, but help us to remember that our families and friends will be watching to see what we truly believe.

We believe in you and your Son. We believe love was your motivation in sending the Savior. We believe in the spirit of Christmas, provided that Spirit is yours. Guide our choices this month; may they reflect our belief and our dependent faith in you.

10

PROPHECIES OF MESSIAH'S LINEAGE

You might expect God's Messiah to come from a long line of Jewish holy men. Surely God would reward the faithful and keep the Messiah's bloodline pure, right?

The lineage of Jesus Christ can be found in the Gospels of Matthew and Luke. Matthew, who wrote primarily to Jews, included an abbreviated record that traced Jesus' family from Abraham to Joseph, Jesus' legal father. Luke traced Jesus' ancestors from Adam to Mary, mother of the Messiah.

In Matthew's account, we find four surprising references to Gentile women: Tamar, Rahab, Ruth, and Bathsheba.[1] Rahab and Tamar were Canaanites, and Ruth was a Moabite. Since Bathsheba was the wife of a Hittite, she was likely Hittite as well.

"In each case," wrote John Hutchison, "a Gentile showed extraordinary faith in contrast to Jews who were greatly lacking in their faith. The faith of Tamar versus that of Judah, of Rahab versus that of the wilderness generation, and of Ruth versus that of the Israelites in the time of the judges were displayed at crucial times . . . Mention of 'the wife of Uriah' rather than her name was probably meant to focus attention on Uriah and his faith in contrast to that of David, Israel's king. Through all this God remained faithful in preserving the Messianic line . . . through godly Gentiles."[2]

Women were not usually mentioned in Jewish genealogies, and Matthew omitted renowned women like Sarah and Rachel. So why did he include the names of four Gentiles?

First, he may have wanted to highlight the difference between their lives before and after faith in the God of Israel. Second, he wanted to celebrate the inclusion of Gentiles into God's plan of salvation. Third, since all the women had unusual marital situations or scandals in their past, Matthew may have wanted to neutralize the first-century rumor about Jesus being an illegitimate child. Finally, Matthew wanted to stress that Jesus did not descend from the priestly tribe of Levi, but from the royal house of David. He had a legitimate claim to the title "King of the Jews."

In the beginning, after Adam and Eve sinned, God declared that from Eve would come a descendant who would smite the tempter (Genesis 3:15).

After the Flood—in which God destroyed every human except righteous Noah, his sons Shem, Ham, Japheth, and their wives— God told Noah that His glory would "dwell in the tents of Shem." That glory would later emanate from Jesus.

Shem was a forefather of Abram, who left Ur, a city in Mesopotamia, and lived the rest of his life in tents:

Then ADONAI said to Abram, "Get going out from your land, and from your relatives, and from your father's house, to the land that I will show you. My heart's desire is to make you into a great nation, to bless you, to make your name great so that you may be a blessing. My desire is to bless those who bless you, but whoever curses you I will curse, and in you all the families of the earth will be blessed."

Genesis 12:1–3

Abram, whose name God later changed to Abraham, had many sons (Genesis 25:1–2), but God said His promise would be fulfilled through Isaac (Genesis 17:19).

Isaac had two sons, though God said His promise would be fulfilled through Jacob, not Esau (Malachi 1:1–3).

Jacob had twelve sons, and God said the promised King would come from Judah (Genesis 49:10).

Judah was not a perfectly righteous man. To sum up the story found in Genesis 38, Judah refused to give Tamar, his twice-widowed daughter-in-law, to his unmarried son so she could have children. Tamar disguised herself as a prostitute, and Judah unknowingly slept with his daughter-in-law. When Judah heard she was pregnant, he was about to have her killed when she revealed the truth: he was the father of her children. "She is more righteous than I," Judah admitted, "since I didn't give her to my son Shelah" (v. 26).

Tamar gave birth to twins, Perez and Zerah. Perez was among those who left Canaan and traveled to Egypt during the time of famine (Genesis 46:12).

Perez fathered Hezron, Hezron fathered Ram, Ram fathered Amminadab, and Amminadab fathered Nahshon. Nahshon led the tribe of Judah when the Israelites came out of Egypt and prepared to enter the Promised Land (Numbers 1:7).

As the children of Israel approached the thick walls of Jericho, Joshua dispatched two men to spy out the massive city. After they stopped at Rahab's place, the king of Jericho heard that strangers had entered her house. He sent warriors to arrest the spies, but Rahab hid them. When the king's men left to search the surrounding countryside, Rahab spoke to the men for whom she had risked her life:

> "So now, please swear to me by ADONAI, since I have dealt kindly with you, that you also will deal kindly with my father's house. Give me a true sign that you will spare the lives of my father, my mother, my brothers, my sisters and all who belong to them, and save our lives from death."
>
> Joshua 2:12–13

Since Rahab's house was built into the wall surrounding the city, the Hebrew spies told her to hang a scarlet cord from her window so the approaching Israelites would know which house was hers. In unwavering faith she obeyed, and after Israel destroyed the city, Rahab and her family became part of the community of Israel.

Nashon, leader of the tribe of Judah, fathered Salmon, and Salmon married Rahab and fathered Boaz.

During a time of famine, Naomi, her husband, and two sons left their home in Bethlehem and lived in Moab. Her sons took

Moabite wives, Orpah and Ruth, and a few years later, both sons and Naomi's husband had died. The famine had ended by that time, so Naomi wished to return to her homeland. Orpah went back to her people, but Ruth traveled with Naomi to Israel.

Ruth had no sexual scandal in her life, but Moabites were not wanted in Israel. Because the tribe's leaders had refused to help the Hebrews when they were on their way to the Promised Land, God had forbidden Moabites from entering the congregation of Israel (Judges 11:17–18; Deuteronomy 23:4).

So why was Ruth accepted? The rabbinic sage Raba reports that Samuel's court decreed that Deuteronomy 23:4 excluded Moabite *men* because the men had refused to help the Israelites, but the women had remained at home. So Ruth was welcomed into the Jewish community.

Boaz and Ruth had a son, Obed, who became the father of Jesse. Jesse fathered eight sons. God said the Messiah would come through the youngest, David, a shepherd and singer who became one of Israel's greatest kings (Psalm 89:3–4; Isaiah 11:1–2).

David is known as "a man after God's own heart," yet he committed adultery and murder to have Bathsheba (2 Samuel 11). As king, David had the power to command a woman to do as he pleased, and he ordered men to bring her to his palace. When she became pregnant with his child, he tried to pass off the baby as her husband's. When that plan failed, David plotted to have Uriah killed. Once he was dead, David married Bathsheba, who not only lost her first husband but also her baby.

Yet from David came Solomon, son of Bathsheba, the king who led Israel to its greatest power and wealth. From Solomon's descendants came Joseph, the legal father of Jesus. Jesus' mother, Mary, descended from Nathan, another of David's sons.

A Moment for Wonder

By studying the human lineage of the Messiah, we see that God can and will use anyone willing to obey Him. None of the men and women in Jesus' family tree were perfect, and some committed grievous sins. But they all believed God, repented, and made a commitment to obey Him.

God is not finished working through imperfect people. He can and will work through us, even with our faults and weaknesses. How? The Bible tells us that if we want to find favor and a good name in the eyes of God and man, we should trust in God with all our hearts, lean not on our own understanding (we should *use* our own understanding, but we should not *lean* on it), and acknowledge God in all our ways. If we are faithful to do these things, then He will make our paths straight (Proverbs 3:4–6). Who knows? Perhaps one day our grandchildren will talk of what God did through us. What a blessing that would be!

Father, we are far from perfect, but if you can use men and women who are battle-scarred and contrite, then we are yours to use. Show us what you would have us do and remind us not to strive for man's perfection, especially at this time of year. If we can impart a smile, a contribution, or a kindness, whisper in our ears and nudge us in the right direction. Our experience of Christmas doesn't have to be picture-perfect so long as it is about you.

:11:

PROPHECIES OF TIMING

Can we know exactly when Jesus was born? We have already mentioned Daniel's prophecy of seventy weeks, which was enough to alert Jewish scholars and eastern magi as they looked for Messiah's coming.

Additional clues can help us with our calculations, but choosing a date involves so many "ifs," "abouts," and conflicting calendars that it's impossible to be definitive.

This is what we do know:

> Now it happened in those days a decree went out from Caesar Augustus to register all the world's inhabitants. This was the first census taken when Quirinius was governor of Syria.
>
> Luke 2:1–2

Publius Sulpicius Quirinius, known as Cyrenius to the Greeks, was governor of Cilicia, which had been annexed to Syria by the time of Jesus' birth. Ten years later, he was appointed governor of Syria a second time, a fact that causes some scholars to place Jesus' birth at a later date.

Augustus ordered *two* censuses during his reign—one in 28 BC and another in 8 BC. Gabriel visited Mary at some point during the latter tax enrollment, so Jesus was born *after* the census was ordered.

Matthew tells us that Jesus was born *before* the death of Herod the Great, which occurred in 4 BC. Josephus tells us that Herod left Jerusalem for Jericho in 5 BC and never returned to the capital city. Since Herod met with the magi in Jerusalem, we know Jesus was born before 5 BC[1], and He may have been up to two years old when the magi arrived.

Are you dizzy yet? One thing we can know: Jesus was probably not born on December 25. Luke 2:8 says the shepherds were keeping flocks outside when Jesus was born, and they would have sheltered their flocks in a sheepfold from the months of November through April. The ewes were pregnant with spring lambs during those chilly months and would need a protected place in which to give birth.

Jerusalem's December temperatures range from 41 to 55 degrees Fahrenheit. Even more significant is the rain. December is a wet month with an average rainfall of 4.1 inches. Being cold is one thing—and sheep *do* wear wool—but being cold *and* wet is not pleasant for humans or good for newborn lambs.

Why, then, do we celebrate on December 25?

For three hundred years after Jesus' resurrection, people did not celebrate Christ's birth at all. They celebrated Easter, which always followed Passover, and January 6 as the day of His baptism. Not until AD 336 was the "Feast of the Nativity" found on a Roman calendar. Pope Julius I set the date for December 25, hoping to absorb the Roman Saturnalia, an eight-day festival to honor the god Saturn. During Saturnalia, gifts were exchanged, all public business halted, and slaves could eat at their masters' tables. The holiday was a time of drunken revelry and unrestrained merrymaking. The people of the Roman Empire decorated their homes and temples with greenery and candles, holly and ivy.

By the early fourth century, with Christianity as the official religion of Rome, Saturnalia had become a celebration of Jesus' Nativity. The people kept the holly and ivy, the candles, and the gift-giving. Slaves could still eat at their masters' tables, but the practice became an exercise in Christian love, not wild excess. Businesses remained closed, and churches marked the birth of Christ. The word *Christmas*, referring to *Christ's mass*, was not used until the late eleventh century.

So when *was* Jesus born, if not during December? Many believe He was born on the first day of the Feast of *Sukkot* or Tabernacles, also known as the "Season of Joy." Sukkot (pronounced *soo-COTE*) is held on the fifteenth through the twenty-first days of the Jewish month of Tishri, which falls in September or October on our calendar. God established this feast to celebrate the fall harvest and commemorate His protection of the Hebrews during their forty years of wandering in the wilderness (Leviticus 23:33–44).

During the Feast of Sukkot, Jewish families live in a temporary booth, a *sukkah*, to symbolize the tents of the wilderness. During the Second Temple period, at the end of the first day's service, the priests and Levites would go to the Court of the Women, where four huge candelabra rested on towering bases. Each candelabrum had four branches topped by large basins in which rested a wick made from old priestly garments. The Levites poured more than seven gallons of pure oil into each basin, then lit the wicks to commemorate the pillar of fire (the Shekinah) that led the Jews through the wilderness. The flames were so intense that people said the light brightened every courtyard in Jerusalem.

Each day of the festival, a priest drew water from the spring of Siloam and carried it to the inner court of the Temple, where he circled the altar. Levites blew the ceremonial silver trumpets while other priests chanted the words of Isaiah: "With joy you will draw water from the wells of salvation" (12:3). On the seventh day, the priest circled the altar seven times, then poured the water over the altar, washing away the blood from the morning sacrifices. Then joy broke loose! Venerable sages juggled lighted torches while others performed somersaults as part of the celebration. The Talmud said that whoever has not been in Jerusalem for this ceremony has not experienced real joy.[2]

The sukkahs evoked the memory of Israel's tabernacle, where God lived among His people before the Temple. The word *tabernacle* can mean *to indwell*, and John used that imagery to describe the birth of Christ: "And the Word became flesh and tabernacled among us. We looked upon His [Shekinah] glory, the glory of the one and only from the Father, full of grace and truth" (John 1:14).

The festival of Sukkot continued for eight days, marked by ceremonies about God's provision, living water, brilliant light, and boundless joy. Do you see pictures and patterns?

A Moment for Wonder

God speaks to us through word pictures. When God told Abraham to take his beloved son, Isaac, to Mount Moriah, He provided us with another picture of what was to come. In Genesis 22 we see Abraham climbing the mountain, gathering wood for a burnt offering and placing the wood on his son's back. The Oral Torah says Abraham took the wood and laid it on Isaac in the same way a cross is laid on the shoulders of one about to be crucified.[3]

Isaac, the child of promise, asked his father, "Where is the lamb for the burnt offering?"

In Hebrew, Abraham replied with these words: **"God will provide for Himself the lamb for the burnt offering is my son."**[4]

The usual translation is, "God will provide for Himself a lamb for a burnt offering, my son" (Genesis 22:8), yet the same words also tell us that God will provide the Lamb, His Son.

That's exactly what He did.

Father, help us to remember that when your Son arrived is not nearly as important as knowing the joy His presence brings—joy that is available to all people.

Open our eyes to new truths in your Word and strengthen our souls to cling to eternal treasures. Thank you for the lessons of Sukkot—the living water, the amazing joy, the brilliant light—because all these things come from you. May they reside within us and spill out onto all those around us at Christmastime and throughout the year.

12

PROPHECIES OF MESSIAH'S PEOPLE

You probably know Jesus was Jewish, but have you realized the full implications of that fact?

We've already seen that Jesus was descended from Abraham, with a few righteous Gentiles tossed into the mix. He was born in the Jews' Promised Land, in Bethlehem, a few miles outside Jerusalem.

Jesus was also born into an observant Jewish family. Mary and Joseph obeyed the Law of Moses, which meant they observed the Sabbath, didn't eat forbidden foods, and celebrated religious festivals including Passover, the Feast of Tabernacles, and the Feast of Atonement. Jesus was circumcised on the eighth day according to the Law, and at that time His name was announced: Yeshua, meaning *salvation*.

I love it when a name fits.

In Nazareth, Jesus grew up without attracting much attention. He had younger brothers and sisters. At some point, after his legal father died, Jesus would have been responsible for helping His mother oversee the betrothals of His siblings. Every Jewish man and woman was expected to marry and raise a family, except for those men who devoted their lives to Torah study.

When He was about thirty, Jesus moved out of the family home in Nazareth and went to Capernaum where He undertook His life's work. He began teaching, and though He taught some unusual truths ("Love your enemies" comes to mind), He also said He didn't come to destroy the Law, but to fulfill it.

He went first to His own people. Some of them followed Him, though not the rich and powerful. It was the poor who flocked to Him first because they lived simple lives and weren't enmeshed in the increasingly complicated system of rules that had eroded the joy of loving and obeying God.

The Old Testament Jews had been given the Law but failed to obey it. After the exile in Babylon, the returning Jews and their descendants became so determined to keep the Law that they added *more* rules, regulations, and stipulations.

The religious leaders deliberately complicated the Law of Moses. They put a "hedge" around it and were mighty pleased with their efforts. Since the Torah decreed "Do not work or carry a burden on the Sabbath," the rabbis asked, "Is travel considered work? How many steps constitute a journey?" Another rabbi postulated, "Leaving the city is travel, but walking within the city is not." They decided that walking 2,000 cubits was allowable, but if you had to travel even farther, you could drop a basket of food at the 2,000-cubit mark, stop and eat, and declare that spot your domicile. Then you would be free to walk another 2,000 cubits.

While the religious rulers finagled and piled on prohibitions with work-arounds, they figured God would be pleased since they were protecting the Law. They wanted God to be pleased with them. They were certainly pleased with themselves.

But the ordinary people, especially those outside Jerusalem, followed the Law, participated in the festivals, and observed Shabbat. They listened to Jesus, who spoke simple words and understood that the day of rest had been created because *people* needed time off, not God.

Jesus healed their sick, gave sight to blind people, and told stories about farmers and shepherds and women who'd lost coins and turned the house upside down to find them. He talked about salt and light and crops. He talked to rich people, poor people, and foreigners. He touched outcasts and wiped tears from weeping faces.

And He did those things while remaining an observant Jew—obeying the bedrock principles of the Law without worrying overmuch about man-made rules. He chose twelve students, rustic men like himself, and though they spent a lot of time bickering, He knew eleven of them would be faithful until their last breaths.

For three and a half years, Yeshua and His followers walked up and down the land of Israel, speaking to anyone who would listen. He fed thousands with a little boy's lunch, calmed a violent storm with a word, and set a record for net-fishing on a lake called Galilee. He made some people happy, and others want to spit fire.

He told people that God wanted their love. What is the kingdom of God? It is the place where God is king. If God is king of your heart, if you love Him enough to obey Him, then the kingdom of God is within you.

His uncomplicated message rocked the religious rulers. What about their authority and carefully constructed rules? When Jesus resurrected a man who'd been dead four days—one day or two, the leaders could have explained the miracle away, but *four*? No denying that one because of the stench—the leaders plotted to have Him arrested by their Temple guards. They would feature Him in a kangaroo trial, charge Him with blasphemy, and stir up the populace. The Roman procurator, who feared nothing as much as a rebellion, could be persuaded to execute the Nazarene to keep the peace.

End of problem . . . except it wasn't. Jesus rose from the dead after three days and was seen by hundreds of people. The simple, unsophisticated men who had been His students became fearless and cared more about spreading the good news than risking their lives.

Those first-century believers changed the world, but later other believers changed the simple worship of God into complicated religion. Some incorporated elements of pagan worship. Others put hedges around simple truths and emphasized man-made rules instead of loving obedience to God.

And far too many Christians began to blame the Jews for Jesus' death. After AD 70, when the Romans toppled every brick in the Temple, utterly destroyed Jerusalem, and scattered the Jews they did not murder, some said it was what the Jews "deserved for killing Jesus."

Oy.

When Hitler killed six million Jews during World War II, some churches refused to come to their aid. Hitler had the audacity to claim he was "doing the Lord's work."[1]

Martin Luther, great reformer of the faith, said awful things about the Jews. Many of the early Church fathers did the same.

In the late fifteenth century, Spain held inquisitions where Jews were given a choice: convert to Christianity or be tortured to death.

Those people forgot an important truth: Jesus was Jewish, and so were the disciples. So were nearly all the members of the early Church.

God said, "Israel is My son, My firstborn" (Exodus 4:22). The Jews are *still* God's chosen people and the apple of His eye (Zechariah 2:12). God will bless those who bless them and curse those who curse them.

Christian antisemitism is more subtle today, yet some believers insist that the Church has replaced the Jews in God's plan. They say the promises made to the Jews have been transferred to the Church.

Oh, my friend, God has *not* abandoned His chosen people. All God's promises to the Jews are intact because He cannot break His unconditional covenants. We Gentiles who believe in Jesus have been grafted onto *their* tree, and we will never replace the children of Israel. Instead, they have suffered (grafting wounds a tree, does it not?) so we might be saved.

A Moment for Wonder

Job was a righteous man who suffered because God allowed Satan to buffet him. Job lost his children, his wealth, and his health. Three who called themselves friends came by to help, but all they did was insist that Job must have done something awful to merit such punishment from God.

What if this is a pattern? What if Job represents Israel?

Israel is a chosen nation who suffered horrible things because God allowed Satan to buffet them. Many who call themselves Christians have insisted that the Jews have done something awful to merit such punishment from God.

No, my friends. The people of Israel were blinded so *we Gentiles could see* (Romans 11:8–11).

God has a plan for His chosen people:

> "Then I will pour out on the house of David and the inhabitants of Jerusalem a spirit of grace and supplication, when they will look toward Me whom they pierced. They will mourn for him as one mourns for an only son and grieve bitterly for him, as one grieves for a firstborn. In that day there will be a great mourning in Jerusalem. . . . In that day a spring will be opened to the house of David and to the inhabitants of Jerusalem to cleanse them from sin and impurity. It will happen in that day"—it is a declaration of Adonai-Tzva'ot—"that I will erase the names of the idols from the land and they will no longer be remembered. . . ."
>
> Zechariah 12:10–13:2

Father, we know the existence of Israel is one of your miracles. Your chosen people have been marked for extermination by their ancient enemies, Haman the Amalekite, the Seleucids, the Nazis, and those who would celebrate today if Israel were wiped off the map.

Help us to bless the children of Abraham. You have blessed the world through the Jews, and they have suffered like no other people on earth. Do not let us be guilty of causing them pain. Guide us to understand, respect, and appreciate their heritage. Teach us to see the Scriptures from a Jewish perspective so we can better understand you.

13

THE PROPHECY OF MELCHIZEDEK

In Psalm 110:1–4, we find yet another prophecy concerning the arrival of the Messiah:

> A psalm of David.
> ADONAI declares to my Lord:
> "Sit at My right hand
> until I make your enemies a footstool for Your feet" (v. 1).
>
> ADONAI has sworn, and will not [change] His mind:
> "You are a Kohen forever according to the order of
> Melchizedek" (v. 4).

God inspired David to write about the coming Messiah. He, Jesus, will sit at God's right hand until His enemies have been brought low. The Messiah will be a priest forever in the order of Melchizedek.

What does the prophecy mean? To understand, we need to review the story of the king of Salem.

He is first mentioned in Genesis 14:1–12. Abram had just rescued his nephew, Lot, from a coalition of enemy kings that had ransacked several cities. On his way home, Abram was greeted by two rulers: Melchizedek, king of Salem (which later became Jeru-salem), and the unnamed king of Sodom.

Melchizedek brought bread and wine to sustain Abram and his men. He was a priest of "God Most High," and he blessed Abram, saying,

> "Blessed be Abram by El Elyon,
> Creator of heaven and earth,
> And blessed be El Elyon,
> Who gave over your enemies into your hand."
>
> Genesis 14:19–20

Abram honored Melchizedek by giving him a tenth of everything he had with him.

Then the king of Sodom, whose city had been pillaged by the enemy coalition, told Abram, "Give me the people—the possessions take for yourself" (Genesis 14:21). In other words, if Abram would return the people taken from Sodom, he could keep all the treasure, animals, and goods taken from that city.

What did Abram do? He accepted the blessing of Melchizedek and then responded to the king of Sodom: "I raise my hand in oath to ADONAI, El Elyon, Creator of heaven and earth. Not a thread or even a sandal strap of all that is yours will I take, so you will not say, 'I've made Abram rich!'" (14:22–23).

Abram returned all the people—including his nephew—who had been taken from Sodom, along with all the goods and livestock.

The writer of Hebrews reminds us of that event:

> For this Melchizedek was king of Salem, kohen [priest] of God
> Most High. He met Abraham returning from the defeat of the
> kings and blessed him, and to him Abraham apportioned a tenth
> of everything. First, by the translation of his name, he is "King of
> Righteousness"; and then also King of Salem, which is "King of
> Shalom [peace]." Without father, without mother, without gene-
> alogy, having neither beginning of days nor end of life but made
> like Ben-Elohim [son of God], he remains a kohen for all time.
>
> Hebrews 7:1–3

For years scholars have debated whether Melchizedek was a
Christ figure or possibly Christ himself. Some point to the fact
that Melchizedek is "without father or mother" as evidence that
this is a preincarnate appearance of Jesus. They argue that the
king of Sodom's offer is similar to Satan's temptation of Jesus, and
the king of Salem's offer of bread and wine is what Jesus offered
His disciples at the Last Supper.

But others believe Melchizedek was a mortal, righteous man
whose genealogy, birth date, and death date were simply unre-
ported in the Scriptures.

". . . all the writer [of Hebrews] was saying is that there is no
genealogy for Melchizedek in Genesis and no record of his death,"
wrote Robert Hughes and Carl Laney. "The absence of this ma-
terial is used by way of analogy with Christ's eternality."[1]

I can't say for certain that Melchizedek was an appearance of
the preincarnate Messiah, but he was certainly a picture of the
Messiah to come. Yet David's prophecy in Psalm 110 is not focused

on Melchizedek's identity; it was meant to show that the coming Messiah would not be like other priests. The Messiah would be a king *and* a priest, One who would never die or be replaced.

Israel was meant to be a kingdom of priests and a holy nation, but Israel and her priests were sinful. Because they weren't holy, the system of sacrifice and atonement enacted by the high priest kept the nation in fellowship with God through the high priest's intervention, who offered a substitutionary sacrifice on their behalf.

But the high priests also needed purification from sin and had to make sacrifices for themselves. "In short," wrote Albert Edersheim, "all this was symbolical (of man's need, God's mercy, and His covenant), and typical, till He should come to whom it all pointed, and who had all along given reality to it; He whose Priesthood was perfect, and who on a perfect altar brought a perfect sacrifice, once for all—a perfect Substitute, and a perfect Mediator."[2]

After Jesus' death and resurrection, no longer would Israel's priests need to follow the Levitical code to atone for sin through sacrifices. The penalty for sin was offered when Jesus the Messiah offered His sinless life to pay for the sins of the world. He paid a debt we could never satisfy, and now forgiveness is available to all who call upon His name.

Moses had instituted the covenant of the Law and its sacrifices. Jesus the Messiah instituted a new covenant for both Jews and Gentiles.

> "Behold, days are coming"
> —it is a declaration of ADONAI—
> "when I will make a new covenant
> with the house of Israel

and with the house of Judah—
not like the covenant
I made with their fathers
in the day I took them by the hand
to bring them out of the land of Egypt. . . ."
Jeremiah 31:30–31

And when He [Jesus] had taken *matzah* [bread] and offered the *bracha* [blessing], He broke it and gave it to them, saying, "This is My body, given for you. Do this in memory of Me." In the same way, He took the cup after the meal, saying, "This cup is the new covenant in My blood, which is poured out for you" (Luke 22:19–20).

Jesus is now the High Priest for all humanity, the Mediator between God and humans. No longer would Israel's high priests die and be replaced, for Jesus is the eternal High Priest, fulfilling the prophecy of Psalm 110: "ADONAI has sworn, and will not change His mind: 'You are a Kohen [priest] forever according to the order of Melchizedek.'"

A Moment for Wonder

In the Old Testament, the people's sins were forgiven on the Day of Atonement. Two goats would be presented to the high priest, and lots were cast to see which goat would be sacrificed and which would be driven into the wilderness (Leviticus 16:7–10, 20–22).

Based on Isaiah 1:18, "Though your sins be like scarlet, they will be as white as snow," the custom was to tie a red sash around the neck of the goat that symbolically carried the people's sins away. According to Talmudic records, the red sash turned white as the goat was driven into the wilderness, a visible sign that God had forgiven Israel's sins.[3]

But the Talmud records an odd event that occurred forty years before the destruction of the Temple—the scapegoat's sash failed to turn white. Why would God not forgive the people's sins in the year AD 30?

Hebrews 10:16–18 provides an answer:

> "After those days," says ADONAI,
> "I will put My Torah upon their hearts,
> and upon their minds I will write it."
> Then He says,
> "I will remember their sins and their lawless deeds no more."
> Now where there is removal of these, there is no longer an
>   offering for sin.

Father, thank you for sending Jesus to be not only our Savior but also our High Priest and Mediator. Thank you for allowing Him to be a perfect human, so He understands our weakness and our failings. Thank you for strengthening Him to be fully God, completely holy and righteous.

You could have sent a king who would rule us by force. You could have sent a priest who would demand that we pay with our own blood. You could have refused to send a savior at all, leaving us to die in our sin. But you saw beyond our stubbornness and weakness. You looked past our pride and arrogance. You saw, above all, our brokenness and need for salvation, and you provided it.

Thank you for sending Jesus at Christmas—our Savior, our King, and our eternal High Priest.

The Prophecies: The Prophet's Job Description

In 1911, a surgeon named Richard Clement Lucas predicted that our "useless" outer toes would become unnecessary, so "man might become a one-toed race." Oy! Because we need all our toes for balance, I suppose he meant the outer four toes would converge into one.[4] Good-bye, pointy shoes!

In 1994, the RAND Corporation, a global think tank, expected animals to be on the payroll by 2020 and theorized it would be possible to breed intelligent animals to perform manual labor like housecleaning and driving the family car.[5] (My dogs vacuum pretty well if food crumbs hit the floor.)

Writer Arthur C. Clark, who cowrote the screenplay for *2001: A Space Odyssey*, believed that by the twenty-first century, our homes would have nothing to keep them on the ground, so they could rise and move anywhere whenever we pleased.[6] We and our houses could fly south for the winter just like the birds.

But you'd still have to reserve a location, wouldn't you? There's not enough room for every snowbird to winter on a Florida beach.

In 1950, the *New York Times* science editor, Waldemar Kaempffert, wrote a *Popular Mechanics* article and predicted that cooking would soon become "only a memory in the minds of old people." He also believed it would be possible to take old table linens and rayon underwear to chemical factories, where they would "be converted into candy."[7]

Um . . . no. Please.

A 1966 edition of *Time* reported that machines would be producing so much in the twenty-first century that everyone in the United States would be independently wealthy. An ordinary non-working family could expect an average salary of about $300,000 (in 2020 dollars) for doing nothing.[8]

I'm no economist, but I am a student of human nature, and I predict that such a scenario would be a recipe for disaster. People need something to do, and while everyone is loafing, who's going to fix the plumbing?

Anyone can create a prediction. Some forecasts come true, and I for one am grateful someone was clever enough to envision a home computer and a mobile phone.

Yet a lot of predictions don't come to pass because they're not based on anything more substantial than desire. I would love to have a house that could park itself in Switzerland for the summer, but the idea of a flying house denies the reality of gravity, matter, and building codes.

A prophecy, on the other hand, is not based on whim or desire, but on the Word of God. A prophet's job is to tell people what God told him to say. If what he says isn't true or doesn't come to pass, he's deemed a false prophet (Deuteronomy 18:18–22).

Prophecy is a spiritual gift, given to certain individuals to aid the Church (1 Corinthians 12:28; Ephesians 4:11). Sometimes a prophecy doesn't involve the future but is a message to help the Church in the present moment. Many pastors have the gift of prophecy and demonstrate it by foretelling or truth-telling when they speak.

Have your family jot down a list of prophecies made in the last five years—you can do an internet search for them. How many of those prophecies have already failed?

Everything a true prophet says will come to pass because God cannot lie. Jesus was a true prophet, Moses as well. All the prophets in the Bible spoke what God told them to speak, and that's why we can trust the Word of God. Every prophecy in the original sixty-six books of the Bible has either already come true or one day will.

PART 3

THE PEOPLE OF CHRISTMAS

14

THE MACCABEES

As Christian families shop and decorate their Christmas trees, observant Jewish families place menorahs in their homes and prepare for the celebration of Hanukkah. Do Hanukkah and Christmas have a connection? They do, for without Hanukkah and the work of God, we would not *have* Christmas.

Jesus celebrated Hanukkah:

> Then came Hanukkah; it was winter in Jerusalem. Yeshua was walking in the Temple around Solomon's Colonnade. Then the Judean leaders surrounded Him, saying, "How long will You hold us in suspense? If You are the Messiah, tell us outright!" Yeshua answered them, "I told you, but you don't believe!"

> John 10:22–25

Hanukkah, also called the Feast of Dedication, honors a series of battles that took place during the four hundred "silent years" between the end of the Old Testament and the beginning of the New. Hanukkah would not exist but for a group of brothers who came to be known as the Maccabees.

After the Jews returned from Babylonian exile, they rebuilt the walls of Jerusalem under Nehemiah. Not all the Jews returned to Israel. Many remained in the East, including Daniel, Esther, and Mordecai, while others settled along the Mediterranean Sea. A large number moved to Egypt.

Daniel had prophesied about world events that soon began to occur: first, the kingdom of Babylon fell to the Medo-Persians. Daniel served Cyrus, king of Persia, and later Esther would marry Ahasuerus, one of his successors. In 323 BC, Alexander the Great conquered the Persian Empire. Shortly thereafter, at age thirty-two, Alexander died and his generals divided his massive kingdom.

Seleucus took charge of the land of Israel, and his successors governed with a heavy hand. Antiochus Epiphanes, who reigned from 175 to 164 BC, invaded Jerusalem, desecrated the Temple by sacrificing a pig on the holy altar, and declared that anyone who observed the Law of Moses would be put to death. To force the Jews to assimilate into Greek culture, he enacted draconian measures. Apparently, he did not realize—or care—that the Jews were meant to be a separate and unique people.

The devout Jews were greatly troubled by the eagerness of other Jews to conform to the Greek lifestyle. This group, who adopted the clothing, philosophies, and language of the Greeks, were known as Hellenes or Hellenists.

Many righteous Jews left Jerusalem and retreated to farming communities. The Seleucid king's representatives visited these settlements and conducted loyalty tests. Those who would not offer sacrifices to Greek gods were executed. In Jerusalem, leading citizens were tested in more subtle ways. At one banquet the host served pork, and those who refused to eat it were arrested, tortured, and killed.

If not for the miracle Hanukkah commemorates, the religious distinctiveness of the Jewish people would have been obliterated.

One family decided to worship the true God alone no matter what the cost. When two Seleucid officials came to their small town and demanded that Mattathias ben Johanan, a Levite, make an offering to a pagan god, Mattathias killed the king's representatives. His five sons took up the cause of righteousness, and the strongest of them, Judah Maccabees, put out a call for men who would fight for the freedom to worship God.

With God's help, Judah and his brothers took a group of untrained farmers and created a guerrilla army. After months of fighting, they defeated a highly trained military force, complete with battle elephants!

When Judah's men recaptured the city of Jerusalem, they went to the Temple Mount and hauled out every stone that had been defiled by the invaders. Once that arduous task was complete, they rebuilt and rededicated the Temple, held a feast, and decreed that an annual Feast of Dedication should be observed so no one would forget how God had preserved His people.

What, then, does Hanukkah have to do with Christmas? During the subsequent period of Hasmonean rule, religious divisions among the Jews deepened. The Pharisees objected to the ruling Hasmoneans (who became Sadducees) because the Hasmonean high priests were descendants of Mattathias's family and not from the line of Aaron. The wealthy and influential Sadducees didn't want to share their power, so they plotted against the Pharisees. The Essenes, sick of the turmoil, retreated into the wilderness and prayed desperately for the arrival of the promised Messiah.

As religious divisions deepened with each passing year, the ordinary people of Jerusalem, most of whom were neither Pharisees or Sadducees, longed for deliverance from bloodshed and deprivation. By the time the Romans declared Judea a Roman province, Messianic yearnings had reached a fever pitch.

As the four hundred "silent years" drew to a close, never had the people of Israel been more ready to welcome their promised Deliverer. Just as God heard their cries when they were enslaved in Egypt, He heard their cries under Seleucid oppression and Roman occupation.

He sent a Deliverer, but not the one they expected.

A Moment for Wonder

When I consider the civilized world at the time of Jesus' birth, I can't help but think of our world today. Divisions among people have never been more pronounced. Despite our technological advances and the wealth of knowledge at our fingertips, our societies are crumbling. We're threatened by large events like nuclear warfare, as well as tiny things—bits of computer code and invisible organisms that can wreck economies, change the course of nations, and kill millions. Our families are fractured, and the wisdom we inherited from our forefathers has been questioned or turned on its head. We don't trust politicians or news reporters because their truth shifts with every cultural breeze.

Believers are often looked at with skepticism or outright loathing because we believe God's Word is not outdated and His standards don't change. People question our loyalties when our convictions conflict with cultural opinions or government regulations. We find ourselves in situations like the Jews in Hellenistic Judea; the purveyors of public opinion don't understand why we can't adapt our convictions to support their beliefs.

Our situation is not as dire as that faced by the people of Israel under Seleucid oppression, but the clock is ticking . . . and hope is born of suffering. We wait, looking toward the sky, because our Messiah is coming again.

Father, you said the world would grow dark in the last days, that scoffers would come, that people would be lovers of self, lovers of money, boastful, arrogant, blasphemers, disobedient to parents, ungrateful, unholy, hardhearted, unforgiving, backbiting, without self-control, brutal, hating what is good, treacherous, reckless, conceited, lovers of pleasure rather than lovers of God, holding to an outward form of godliness but denying its power.

Yet you sent the Light of the World into such darkness, and He shone so brightly that our world was forever changed. Help us reflect that light in our corrupted society and remind us that we carry His glory within us to illuminate dark places. Give us courage and help us to hold fast to the truth of your Word. Remind us that as long as the Light shines, darkness will not and cannot prevail.

15

ZECHARIAH

For over forty years, Zechariah had made the pilgrimage from Juttah to Jerusalem so he could serve his course in the Temple. Now, in the autumn of his life, his spirit had wearied of the journey.

He and his wife, Elizabeth, had lived blameless lives before God and man, observing the commands and ordinances of Adonai, and for what? He had never been chosen to serve in the Holy Place.

And Elizabeth had never been blessed with a child.

Despite their many prayers, despite their devotion to Adonai and the Law, Zechariah and his wife thought they would die poor and childless. His neighbors called him doubly blessed, for he was a *cohen* from the order of Abijah, and Elizabeth had descended from the order of Aaron. But of what use was a godly heritage if a man could not bequeath it to sons and daughters?

Now Zechariah stood with the other Levites in the Chamber of Hewn Stone. The prayers concluded, and the leader set about choosing the priests who would serve in the Holy Place.

The leader signaled for the Levites to remove their head coverings. Since the Law forbade the counting of persons, the leader would begin with the oldest priest and count upraised fingers. Some men held up four fingers, others two or three.

The leader counted off two lots. The first selected a priest to cleanse and prepare the altar. The second designated the priest who would approach the Holy Place to offer the sacrifice, trim the candlestick, and clear the sacred stone.

The leader prepared to choose the priest who would perform the most important task, the offering of incense. Those who had previously been granted that honor discreetly backed out of the circle. The privilege of offering the incense could not be repeated in a priest's lifetime.

Zechariah was the oldest man remaining. Like a virgin daughter for whom no man asks, he stood with the younger priests, lifted a single finger, and waited once again for the Spirit of Adonai to move in the casting of lots.

The leader announced a random number—seventy-one—and fingers fluttered and settled as he counted again, moving swiftly around the circle of upraised hands.

"Sixty-eight, sixty-nine, seventy . . . seventy-one."

Zechariah's throat went dry when the leader's bulky form filled his field of vision. "You, Zechariah." Awe filled the man's voice, not for the chosen cohen but out of respect for the honor. "HaShem, blessed be He, has chosen you to offer incense before the altar."

Zechariah nodded, not certain he could trust his voice. More than fifty cohanim stood with him, yet *he* had been selected to perform this most important task.[1] Why now?

God moved through location, time, and the casting of lots to bring Zechariah to the place where he was meant to be.

Zechariah's job would be to hold the golden censer and wait until the worship leader proclaimed that the time of incense had come. Then he would step into the Holy Place and arrange the incense on the altar. As the fragrant cloud rose toward heaven, Zechariah would bow and retreat, head down, as the people in the courtyard chanted praise. He would then turn at the top of the stairs and give the traditional benediction.

He was ready.

"The time of incense has come!" As the worship leader's cry echoed above the shuffle of kneeling bodies, Zechariah stepped forward. He spread incense on the hot coals and exhaled slowly as a spiral of smoke rose into the sacred space. Along with the leader, he whispered prayers as white plumes swirled before him . . .

They represented the heartfelt prayers of his people. His prayers and Elizabeth's.

He was lowering the empty censer, preparing to leave the Holy Place, when something moved in the smoke.

"Zechariah."

Zechariah stiffened. The Shekinah had spoken to Moses from the altar of incense, but this couldn't be the voice of God, for God hadn't spoken, even through his prophets, in over four hundred years.

"Zechariah."

The voice filled the space around the altar, speaking his name.

Zechariah peered into the swirling smoke.

The voice belonged to the angel Gabriel, the same messenger who would later appear to Mary. He said that Zechariah and Elizabeth would soon have a son, and they were to name him John. "And you will have joy and gladness, and many will rejoice at his birth.

He will be great before ADONAI. . . . And he will go before Him in the spirit and power of Elijah, to turn the hearts of fathers to the children and the disobedient ones to the wisdom of the righteous, to make ready for ADONAI a prepared people" (Luke 1:14–17).

God hadn't spoken through His prophets in generations. The worship of Adonai had evolved into a series of rituals based on the Law given to Moses on Sinai. But the religious leaders and Torah teachers had become experts at complicating the Law. By the dawn of the first century, the worship of God had become so difficult that many in Israel didn't even bother to try. The Pharisees made a life's work out of obeying every jot and tittle of their convoluted Law and shunning everyone who didn't share their obsession. The average man in Israel tried to respect the Sabbath, attend the pilgrimage festivals when he could, and keep the Ten Commands.

Even Zechariah had grown cynical. After hearing the angel's news, he said, "How will I know this for certain? I'm an old man, and my wife is well-advanced in age."

After seeing the archangel Gabriel, after winning the lottery of a Levite's lifetime, after being in the right place at the preordained moment, Zechariah wanted *assurance*?

"I am Gabriel, the one standing in God's presence," the archangel replied. "I was commissioned to tell you and proclaim to you this good news. So look, you will be silent and powerless to speak until the day these things happen, since you did not believe my words which will be fulfilled in their time" (Luke 1:18–20).

Scripture does not record what Zechariah felt when his wife's belly swelled with the promised new life. How did he communicate the news of his visitation to her? Did he write out the story? How did Elizabeth react?

And how did the Levite feel when young Mary, the girl chosen to bear the Messiah, arrived at his house for a visit? Elizabeth knew about the miracle growing in Mary's virgin womb and did not question the unbelievable news. As Zechariah watched the two women celebrate and lift their voices in praise to Adonai, did he chide himself for his initial unbelief?

I'm sure the two women, both carrying miracle children, spent many hours praying and praising God, who was doing a mighty work in their midst. Zechariah must have looked on, silent and still, marveling that God had chosen him, his wife, and his wife's young relative to deliver the Messiah for whom His people had been waiting such a long time.

By the time Elizabeth gave birth to the one chosen to prepare the way for the Hope of the World, Zechariah had repented of his disbelief. On the day of the baby's circumcision, Zechariah announced the child's name and used his voice for the first time in months: "Blessed be ADONAI, God of Israel," he said, "for He has looked after His people and brought them redemption" (Luke 1:68).

In a season of cynicism, Zechariah saw the light.

A Moment for Wonder

How many times has God put us in the right place at the preordained time, sent a godly brother or sister to give us guidance, and we responded with "Are you sure about that?"

God delights in using ordinary people in extraordinary ways, and He wants to use us. The twelve men Jesus chose for His disciples were ordinary at the start, yet they became extraordinary through the power of the Holy Spirit.

Gideon must have thought it a joke when the Angel of the Lord sat under an oak tree, looked up at him, and said, "ADONAI is with you, O mighty man of valor." Mighty man of *what*? Gideon was a farmer, and though he had heard of God's mighty acts on behalf of the people of Israel, he had never seen a miracle. He pointed out that inconvenient truth.

"Then ADONAI turned toward him and said, 'Go in this might of yours and deliver Israel from the hand of Midian. Have not I sent you?'" (Judges 6:14).

In this might of yours . . . Within Gideon, God saw what others— even Gideon—could not. If God leads you to do something, He will supply the strength, courage, and support you need for the task.

As God spoke to Israel, He speaks to believers today: "For I know the plans that I have in mind for you," declares ADONAI, "plans for *shalom* and not calamity—to give you a future and a hope. Then you will call on Me, and come and pray to Me, and I will listen to you. You will seek Me and find Me, when you will search for Me with all your heart" (Jeremiah 29:11–13).

Father, Zechariah had every reason to consider himself less than ordinary until you called him to the unique task of parenting John the Baptist. Since you exist beyond the boundaries of time, you have always known what he would do and how he and

Elizabeth would nurture the one who would prepare Israel for her Messiah.

You know the plans you have for us. Equip us for those plans and remind us to fervently search for you. When we call on you, teach us the lessons we'll need in those all-important moments when we, even unknowingly, impact eternity.

16

JOHN THE BAPTIZER

In ancient times, a herald would run before the chariot of the king, alerting people to his approach. When they heard the herald's shout, people would stop what they were doing and prepare to bow. If they were doing something the king wouldn't approve of, they'd adjust their behavior.

John the Baptist was the herald for the promised King of the Jews. When John began to preach, people stopped what they were doing to listen, and a great many of them repented of their ungodly actions to prepare themselves for the Messiah.

When Elizabeth gave birth to her baby, her family and neighbors rejoiced because she who had been barren had been blessed with a son. On the eighth day, when the time came for the child to be named and circumcised, Elizabeth said the child would be named John. Actually, his Hebrew name was *Yochanan*, pronounced YOK-ah-nun.

Her announcement stunned the friends and family who had gathered to celebrate the child's name-day because no one in either Elizabeth's or Zechariah's family was named Yochanan.

The guests protested that she was defying tradition, but Elizabeth refused to relent.

The guests turned to Zechariah, who had been mute ever since his encounter with the archangel Gabriel. He must have been rendered deaf as well because the guests made signs to him instead of *telling* him about the problem (Luke 1:62).

After asking for a tablet, Zechariah wrote the words, *His name is Yochanan.*

End of story.

He and Elizabeth were committed to obeying God, who had already supplied the baby's name. Because Zechariah was obedient, in that moment his speech and hearing were restored. He immediately began to praise God and prophesy.

Zechariah's prophecy focused on his son and the coming Messiah. The first part of his declaration (Luke 1:68–75) speaks of the Messiah's salvation. The second half centers on John's ministry.

Perhaps he held his tiny son in his arms as he uttered these words:

> "And you, child, will be called a prophet of Elyon
>   [the Most High].
> For you will go before ADONAI to prepare His ways,
> to give knowledge of salvation to His people
> through removal of their sins.
> Through our God's heart of mercy,
> the Sunrise from on high will come upon us,
> to give light to those who sit in darkness
> and in the shadow of death,
> to guide our feet in the way of shalom."
>
> Luke 1:76–79

Because God's heart overflows with mercy, "the Sunrise from on high will come"—a reference to Malachi 3:20: "But for you who revere My Name, the sun of righteousness will rise, with healing in its wings." This Sun will shine on two groups: those who sit in spiritual darkness (the Gentiles), and the Jews, to whom the Messiah will bring peace.[1]

We know very little about John's youth, but we do know he went to the desert early in his life and lived there "until the day of his public appearance to Israel" (Luke 1:80). John was the divinely appointed herald, and what happened to the herald, says rabbi Arnold Fruchtenbaum, would also happen to the King.[2] Another pattern.

Gabriel announced the impending birth of both men.

Both babies were borne by women who should not have been able to have children.

Both were named by God.

Both spent time in the wilderness.

Both waited until the Spirit led them to begin public ministry.

John preached on the east bank of the Jordan River, just before it joined the Dead Sea. Because the river was too shallow to immerse people in the dry season, John moved north to Aenon near Salim, for "much water was there" in that location (John 3:23).

When John told the people to repent, they asked, "How? What shall we do?"

John's answer was nothing if not practical. "Whoever has two coats, let him give to the one who has none," he said, "and whoever has food, let him do the same."

To the tax collectors he said, "Do not take more than you are supposed to."

He admonished soldiers, "Do not take things from anyone by force, do not falsely accuse anyone, and be content with your wages" (Luke 3:10–14).

When John's disciples became concerned that Jesus was baptizing more people than their master, they went to John. He allayed their fears, explaining that the situation was unfolding as God intended. "You yourselves testify that I said, 'I am not the Messiah,' but rather, 'I am sent before Him.' The one who has the bride is the bridegroom, but the best man rejoices when he stands and hears the bridegroom's voice. So now my joy is complete! He must increase, while I must decrease" (John 3:28–30).

John understood exactly who he was meant to be.

A Moment for Wonder

What happened to the herald, happened to the King.

Both John and Jesus attracted students (disciples).

Both men ministered for a period of approximately three years. John likely spent two of those years in Antipas's prison.

Both John and Jesus spoke the truth, and some people hated them for it.

Both were arrested while innocent.

Both were put to death for personal reasons disguised as political actions.

You may be familiar with the story of John's execution. Herod Antipas had married Herodias, the former wife of his still-living brother. Such a marriage was forbidden by Jewish law, and John didn't hesitate to call out the couple's sin. Antipas was afraid to act because he knew John was a righteous man, but Herodias jumped at an opportunity to kill the prophet who had criticized her.

At Antipas's birthday party, Herodias's daughter Salome danced for the king. Antipas was so pleased that he recklessly promised the girl anything she wanted. Prompted by her vengeful mother, Salome asked for the head of John the Baptist on a platter, and Antipas ruefully granted her request.

John's disciples were allowed to take the prophet's body and place it in a tomb, and afterward they informed Jesus of his relative's death (Matthew 14:12).

John died after he completed his mission. And of him Jesus said, "Amen, I tell you, among those born of women, none has arisen greater than John the Immerser. Yet the least in the kingdom of heaven is greater than he" (Matthew 11:11).

Father, as Jesus is coming again, may we be heralds of the returning King. John spoke to people living in darkness, those who were not so different from people living today. John testified of his Kinsman, the coming Messiah, and we who have been made sons and daughters of God can testify of our Lord's return.

Help us to speak as openly and plainly as John did. Help us to be on guard against those who would stifle our speech or twist our message. Protect us from the evil one. You have called us to be witnesses, so give us the strength and wisdom to be faithful heralds.

:17:

MARY OF NAZARETH

Her real name was Miriam, and though hundreds of books have been written about her, the Bible gives us only a brief sketch of the girl from Galilee. Like hundreds of young Jewish women, she had been named after the sister of Moses. The name either comes from the Egyptian word for *beloved* or the Hebrew word for *rebel*. Considering the name's popularity and that Moses' sister was born in Egypt, *beloved* is the most likely meaning.

Mary was probably a young teenager when the archangel Gabriel visited her. In that era, many girls were betrothed as youngsters, but they were not married until after they were capable of bearing children. Mary was most likely between the ages of thirteen and seventeen when the angel appeared to her.

Physical immaturity wasn't the only reason for postponing a marriage. Most grooms didn't claim their brides until they'd finished building a home for their new families. This home would often be attached to the groom's father's dwelling.

Since Joseph was a builder, perhaps he was waiting to finish his house, or perhaps he was waiting to finish *other* people's houses so he could begin his own.

Mary, an ordinary girl, was chosen by God for an exceptional mission: she would be the mother of the Messiah. She was "highly favored," *kecharitomene* in Greek, meaning *I favor*. She wasn't granted special favor because she deserved it any more than we were granted salvation because we were deserving. God granted Mary favor—and us salvation—because *He chose to do it*.[1]

As a teenager, Mary agreed to perform a difficult task—present herself to her family, friends, and fiancé with an unexpected pregnancy and an astounding explanation.

Consider all the men who balked when God asked them to do something. Moses protested that he didn't have a smooth tongue. Gideon said he was the least capable fellow in his family. Jonah fled on a ship. But when Gabriel told Mary she would bear the long-awaited Messiah, Mary said, "I am the Lord's servant."

Gabriel mentioned that Mary's older relative, Elizabeth, was also expecting a miracle baby. Her son, conceived after years of infertility, was filled with the Holy Spirit even before his birth. When Mary visited Elizabeth after Gabriel's announcement, Elizabeth's six-month-old fetus recognized the voice of the holy child's mother (Luke 1:42–45). Elizabeth also knew Mary's secret, even though the unborn Savior was probably smaller than a pea.

At that point, Mary understood only *part* of God's plan for her Son. She knew God had worked a miracle in her womb. She knew she would be called "blessed" by future generations. She knew her Son would fulfill promises God made to Abraham and the people of Israel. But like most of us, she did not know what the future would bring. She didn't even know if she would survive childbirth.

Nevertheless, she trusted God. She faced several risks. First, under Mosaic Law, a pregnant, unmarried woman could have been put to death by the religious leaders. Second, the community could have expelled her from the synagogue and the town. And third, Joseph could have publicly shamed and divorced her, turning the entire town against her.

But Mary trusted the Lord to handle her fears. And after hearing from an angel in a dream, Joseph took her into his home, which alleviated her other concerns.

Mary remained humble after giving birth. When she met Simeon and Anna at her purification ceremony in the Temple, Mary learned her Son would face opposition. She learned that "a sword" would pierce her soul (Luke 2:34–35). She might have noticed that Simeon spoke to her *alone* when he mentioned the sword; he did not address Joseph.

Though Mary had been granted a unique joy, she would also suffer a unique grief.

Matthew 1:24 tells us that Joseph didn't know Mary intimately until after Jesus had been born, implying that they *did* consummate their marriage after the birth of the holy child. Luke 2:7 lets us know that Jesus was Mary's firstborn son, implying she had other sons later.

When twelve-year-old Jesus went missing after a trip to Jerusalem, His parents found Him at the Temple. Panic-stricken after three days of searching, Mary said, "Child, why did you do this to us? Look! Your father and I were searching for You frantically!"

"Why were you searching for Me?" Jesus asked them. "Didn't you know that I must be about the things of My Father?" (Luke 2:48–49).

Mary must have drawn a deep breath, silenced her urge to scold Him, and reminded herself: *I am the Lord's servant.*

When at age thirty Jesus left the family home and moved to Capernaum to begin His ministry, Mary watched Him go, blinking back tears as she told herself: *I am the Lord's servant.*

After beginning his work, Jesus returned to speak at Nazareth's synagogue. When he had finished, the people asked themselves, "Isn't this the carpenter's son? Isn't His mother called Miriam, and His brothers Jacob and Joseph and Simon and Judah? And His sisters, aren't they all with us?" (Matthew 13:55).

We don't know if Jesus' brothers were in the synagogue that day, but they were nowhere in sight when Jesus' listeners became so incensed they nearly threw Him over a cliff. Mary might have remained sitting in the women's section, remembering the lesson she'd be learning all her life: *I am the Lord's servant.*

Later, when Mary heard about what had happened at the court of Jerusalem's Great Sanhedrin, where paid informants lied and contradicted each other in testimony about her Son, she bowed her head in sorrowful silence. *I am the Lord's servant.*

And when she stood in front of her Son's cross, deserted by all but a few, she watched His face contort in agony and His lifeblood ebb away. When He said, "Woman, behold your son," indicating that she should leave with John, everything within her wanted to refuse, but she did not. Because she was *the Lord's servant.*

Mary suffered an agony unlike any other, yet she did not question God's will. "Behold, the servant of ADONAI," she must have whispered time and time again. "Let it be done to me according to your word" (Luke 1:38).

A Moment for Wonder

This Christmas, as we set up our Nativity scenes and think about Mary, we should remember that her task was not a nine-month gig, but a lifetime commitment.

Along with Joseph, Mary surely felt responsible for keeping Jesus safe, guiding His youthful choices, and teaching Him about the things that mattered most. Along the way, she learned to let go. Her Son was not hers alone, so she could not cling to Him.

Are we clinging to things we should release to God? Old memories, expectations, selfish attitudes, or grudges?

After the resurrection, Mary served as a repository of memories for the men who wrote the Gospels. She shared all the stories she had treasured in her heart, serving as a source of knowledge for the disciples and a fount of encouragement for new believers. Most of all, she served as an example of complete, unwavering faithfulness to God's calling.

Surely we should do the same.

Father, please give us the strength to practice Mary's courage, faith, and steadfast loyalty to you. When things are going well, help us to demonstrate her sense of eager expectation; when we are suffering, help us to model her confident faith that you, our sovereign God, have promised to love, hold, and keep us until the pain subsides . . . and afterward.

Most of all, Lord, help us to model Mary's humility, for we are your servants.

:18:

JOSEPH THE BUILDER

Joseph is the unsung hero of the Christmas story. Who was this young man of whom so much was asked?

Scripture doesn't tell us much about Joseph, and not a single word from his lips is recorded in the Gospels. Still, we know Joseph was a descendant of King David and he was betrothed to Mary. He would probably have been between the ages of eighteen and twenty, and the betrothal would have been arranged by both sets of parents with Mary's and Joseph's consent. Since premarital privacy was frowned upon in Galilee, we can assume Mary and Joseph hadn't spent much, if any, unchaperoned time together.

We traditionally think of Joseph as a carpenter, but the Greek word to describe Joseph's job is *tekton*, a man skilled in carpentry, stone masonry, and engraving. A master builder was an *architektonos* from which we get the word *architect*.

A tekton would be hired to do work ordinary people couldn't manage such as setting the corners of a house, aligning the walls to support the roof, building the doors and locks, and overseeing the construction process. The tekton, according to Paul Wright, would be "part builder, part architect, part contractor, and part artisan."[1]

We don't know how Joseph met Mary or if they knew each other well, but during their betrothal period, Mary abruptly left Nazareth and went to visit her kinswoman, Elizabeth. Mary remained in Juttah from Elizabeth's sixth month until her ninth, perhaps even until John's birth.

When Mary returned to Nazareth, she would have been about three months pregnant. Scripture says, "she was found to be pregnant through the *Ruach ha-Kodesh* [the Holy Spirit]" (Matthew 1:18), which seems to suggest she had a baby bump—proving she was truly with child. Mary told her parents about Gabriel's visit, and she told Joseph, her legal husband.

After Mary's shocking revelation, Joseph considered whether to break their betrothal contract. He didn't doubt her pregnancy, and soon everyone in Nazareth would see the evidence of her swelling belly. But could she really be pregnant from the Holy Spirit? No one had ever heard of such a thing!

The betrothal contract was legally and morally binding. If Joseph publicly testified that Mary became pregnant by another man, she could be stoned as an adulteress.

Matthew 1:19 tells us that Joseph, "being a righteous man and not wanting to disgrace her publicly, made up his mind to dismiss her secretly."

After Joseph pondered his dilemma, an angel of the Lord appeared to him in a dream, saying, "Joseph son of David, do not be afraid to take Miriam as your wife, for the Child conceived in her is from the *Ruach ha-Kodesh*. She will give birth to a son; and you shall call His name Yeshua, for He will save His people from their sins" (Matthew 1:20–21).

When Joseph awoke, he went unashamed to Mary's house, claimed her as his bride, and took her home. Later, everyone in Nazareth must have believed Mary was pregnant with Joseph's child. Why else would he have gone ahead with the betrothal? But Scripture assures us that Joseph and Mary had no physical union until after she'd given birth to her Son (Matthew 1:24–25).

On the road to Bethlehem, Joseph cared for Mary, finding her a safe place to ride (probably in a wagon), making sure she had shade and plenty of water, and urging her to put her feet up when her ankles swelled. Once they arrived in Bethlehem, Joseph might have gone from door to door, hoping to find a house with an empty guest room. His frustration must have boiled over when Mary cried out in anguish because the baby was coming.

We'll never know how Joseph convinced a family to let him use their ground floor stable as a labor-and-delivery room, but he did. He helped Mary get comfortable, laid fresh straw in the manger, and shooed the animals away. Then he either helped deliver the child or went in search of a woman who could act as midwife.

Months later, after the magi delivered gifts of gold, frankincense, and myrrh, Joseph went to sleep, and again the angel appeared in his dream. "Get up!" the angel commanded. "Take the Child and His mother and flee to Egypt. Stay there until I tell you, for Herod is about to search for the Child, to kill Him" (Matthew 2:13).

Joseph rolled out of bed, woke Mary and the baby, gathered their few possessions and left for Egypt. Can you imagine the urgency that fired his blood? The wise men's gifts were an unexpected blessing because those treasures would not only finance their journey but would also enable them to survive until he could find work in Egypt. Joseph must have known that a sizable Jewish community existed in Alexandria, so they might have found shelter there.

Joseph had to arrange transportation, trek through the desert, enter a foreign country, and support his young family while they waited, all while not knowing when it would be safe to return to Israel. I'm sure there were occasions when he wondered if he would ever again see his friends and family. Even so, he remained obedient, and when the angel told him the danger had passed, Joseph took his family back to Nazareth.

As a dutiful father, Joseph would have taught Jesus the Torah as a young boy. From the age of six, Jesus would have gone to the synagogue's *bet sefer* (elementary school) and then to the *bet midrash* (secondary school). But Jesus learned—or already knew— truths far beyond men's ability to teach Him. By the time He was twelve, He knew who He was, who His Father was, and how to amaze the Torah teachers at the Temple.

Scripture relates the story of the family's trip to Jerusalem in Jesus' twelfth year. After spending a full day on the road back to Nazareth, Joseph and Mary realized Jesus wasn't among the other children, friends, or family, so they hurried back to Jerusalem.

They found their Son at the Temple, talking to the Torah teachers and being busy "about His Father's business."

Such words spoken from the lips of a twelve-year-old must have startled Joseph. The boy he considered a son had pulled away from the family to fulfill His holy calling. That might have been the moment Joseph realized Jesus would never take over the family business.

How did twelve-year-old Jesus know so much more than the average Torah student? Many believe the answer lies in this prophecy:

> *Adonai Elohim* has given Me the tongue of the learned,
> that I may know how to sustain the weary with a word.
> He awakens Me morning by morning.
> He awakens My ear to give heed as a disciple.
> *Adonai Elohim* has opened My ear,
> and I was not rebellious,
> nor did I turn back.
> I gave My back to those who strike,
> and My cheeks to those pulling out My beard;
> I did not hide My face
> from humiliation and spitting.
> For *Adonai Elohim* will help Me.
> Therefore I have not been disgraced.
> Therefore I set My face like flint,
> and I know that I will not be ashamed.

> Isaiah 50:4–7

A Moment for Wonder

History has inadvertently shed some light on possibilities about Joseph's life. Sepphoris, a Gentile city four miles from Nazareth, was only a two-hour journey away. Herod the Great had considered Sepphoris the capital of Galilee, and soon after his death, Jewish rebels attacked the city. Rome punished the rebels by razing the settlement, but Herod Antipas, who had inherited the right to rule the region, rebuilt Sepphoris, determined to make it the "ornament of all Galilee."

As expert builders, Joseph and Jesus probably spent time working in Sepphoris. Paul Wright says that if Joseph and young Jesus sought employment there, they would not only have found good jobs but they also would have been "exposed to a cultural and ethnic world much larger than that of Nazareth. It also gives a realistic context to many of Jesus' teachings that reference structures and construction techniques."[2]

This gives new meaning to Jesus' story about the man who built his house upon a rock, doesn't it?

Joseph probably died before Jesus began His public work. Scripture tells us nothing more about Joseph after the incident at the Temple, and apparently he was not present during Jesus' ministry. Simeon had warned Mary that a sword would pierce her soul, but since he didn't address Joseph, perhaps Joseph realized he wouldn't live to see the fulfillment of Jesus' mission.

Though the details of Joseph's life are a mystery, we know he was righteous, faithful, and courageous. Whenever God commanded him, he acted quickly in steadfast faith.

Father, as we move through the Christmas season, may we emulate Joseph's understanding, patience, and willingness to do whatever you command without protest or question. Help us to study the Scriptures as he did, so that we'll be able to give an answer to anyone who asks why we believe in you.

19

THE SHEPHERDS
AND ANGELS

When I began researching my novel *The Shepherd's Wife*, I was surprised to discover that few first-century families in Israel kept sheep. I had assumed most families kept livestock because Jesus told so many stories about sheep, lambs, and shepherds.

I then learned that at the time, arable land was too precious to designate for farm animals because it was needed to grow crops. Families or communities might keep a few chickens and a goat for milk and cheese, but few folks kept flocks of sheep.[1]

The land of Israel was divided into regions: Judea was the southernmost region around Jerusalem, Galilee lay to the north, and Samaria was sandwiched between. In Judea, only one area was designated for livestock. The rocky hills outside Jerusalem were reserved for sheep, oxen, and goats because those animals were necessary for Temple sacrifices. When they weren't in the fields, the shepherds lived in Bethlehem.

In the middle of the shepherd's field stood a tower: Migdal-eder, literally *Tower of the Flock*. From this elevated point, the shepherds could look out over the fields and keep watch over the animals. The priests required two one-year-old lambs for daily sacrifices, and many more during the festivals, so the shepherds would herd the necessary animals to the Temple. Worshipers could also make personal sacrifices, so animals for that purpose were sold outside the Temple.

Though the shepherds provided a useful and necessary service, they were on the bottom rung of the social ladder. According to the Law, a person became ritually unclean if he touched a dead person or animal, ate a forbidden food, had a discharge of bodily fluids, or had leprosy. To be made ritually clean, they had to wait a certain number of days, bathe in a *mikveh*, and make a sacrificial offering.

Shepherds and tanners were almost always unclean because they were in frequent contact with dead or sick animals. They were forbidden to enter the Temple in a state of ritual uncleanness, and no one could touch them without becoming unclean themselves. So extreme was the prejudice against shepherds that they were considered liars and not allowed to bear witness in a court of law.

But when Jesus was born, our merciful God sent holy messengers, not to kings or priests, but to *shepherds*. He didn't consider their wealth, social position, or physical appearance. He didn't care that they had grime under their fingernails and smelled of beasts. He looked out at those fields, saw the lowliest of the low, and sent heralds to invite them to meet the newborn king *before anyone else*.

Who were the heavenly messengers? They were angels, but not the sort you see in a gift shop. They were not female, nor did they have wings and wear frilly robes. Seraphim and cherubim have wings, but seraphim have six wings and cherubim leonine bodies. I've never seen *those* in gift shops.

Angels were created by God before the creation of our world, so they aren't the spirits of dead humans. Humans never become angels, and angels have never been human.

The chief duty of an angel is to worship and serve God. Some are warriors who defend God's people; others serve as guardians. Still others are messengers.

A messenger angel appeared to the shepherds. He might have crossed a field and walked up to them, or he might have materialized out of the night air. He might have even passed for human, yet the brilliant Shekinah glory surrounding him assured the shepherds this was no ordinary visitor. The dazzling sight terrified them.

The angel said, "Do not be afraid! For behold, I proclaim Good News to you, which will be great joy to all the people. A Savior is born to you today in the city of David, who is Messiah the Lord. And the sign to you is this: You will find an infant wrapped in strips of cloth and lying in a manger" (Luke 2:10–12).

Then the real excitement began:

And suddenly a multitude of heavenly armies appeared with the angel, praising God and saying, "Glory to God in the highest, and on earth shalom to men of good will."

Luke 2:13–14

The shepherds probably went from terrified to apoplectic, but they didn't move until the angels had departed "into the heavens." When the shepherds finally found their voices, they said, "Let's go to Bethlehem and see this thing that has happened which ADONAI has made known to us!" (Luke 2:15).

Nowhere does the Bible mention an unusual star over Bethlehem that night. The shepherds didn't need a star; they had been given directions. They weren't told to look for a king, but for the Messiah lying in a manger.

A Moment for Wonder

What did the shepherds do after hearing this amazing news? They ran out to find Jesus, then returned to their fields, wide awake with excitement. The next day they spread the news when they delivered the day's sacrificial animals to the Temple courtyard. The prophet Simeon, who would meet the infant Jesus forty days later, may have heard their report, along with Anna the prophetess. Those two waited patiently, eager to greet the newborn king on His presentation day.

The story of that baby has now been shared with every known nation and people. It has been shouted, sung, and broadcast to every continent and from outer space. Everyone who hears the story must decide: will they seek the Savior or remain where they are? And if they seek the Savior and find Him, will they share the story?

On Christmas Eve, 1968, Bill Anders, Jim Lovell, and Frank Borman, the crew of Apollo 8, read aloud from the first chapter of Genesis while in outer space (1:1–10), proclaiming that "In the beginning God created the heavens and the earth . . ."

As you celebrate Christmas this year, look for occasions where you can share the reasons for Messiah's birth. Your holiday cards, decorations, and the traditions you observe—with each choice, you can share the same story the angels proclaimed to a band of shepherds.

God gives everyone a voice . . . and a choice. Ask the Lord to show you how you can use both to honor Him this Christmas.

Father, your goodness never ceases to astound us. You always do the opposite of what we would presume, yet your plan is always best.

Help us to proclaim the true meaning of Christmas this year in every gift, meal, and decoration. Then, in your perfect timing, remind us to share the news about the Messiah in the manger.

20

HEROD AND THE MAGI

How many times have we sung "We Three Kings"? Tradition calls them Caspar, Melchior, and Balthazar, but the biblical account doesn't name them, count them, or even refer to them as kings. Still, they were the first Gentiles to honor and worship the Jews' Messiah.

"Where is the One who has been born King of the Jews?" they asked. "For we saw His star in the east and have come to worship Him" (Matthew 2:2).

As was proper when visiting a king, the wise men brought tributes with them: gold, frankincense, and myrrh. Some believe this was the prophetic fulfillment of Isaiah 60:1–3, 6:

Arise, shine, for your light has come! The glory of ADONAI has risen on you. For behold, darkness covers the earth, and deep darkness the peoples. But ADONAI will arise upon you, and His glory will appear over you. Nations will come to your light, kings to the brilliance of your rising. . . . A multitude of camels will cover you, young camels of Midian and Ephah, all those from Sheba will come. They will bring gold and frankincense, and proclaim the praises of ADONAI.

For safety's sake, the magi would have traveled with a sizable entourage, including several camels carrying water, food, and tents for the journey. Their arrival in Jerusalem certainly caused a stir, as did their persistent question: "Where can we find the newborn King of the Jews?"

Herod, the current king, had a case of paranoia. He wasn't a legitimate Jewish king; he'd been appointed by Rome. He wasn't one of David's heirs; in fact, he'd descended from Esau, not Jacob, and his piety had more to do with public relations than with spiritual commitment.

No wonder the Jews resented him. Herod's lifestyle was unabashedly decadent, and it appeared he was more loyal to Rome than to the Jews. After the Roman Senate declared Herod king of Judea, he married the granddaughter of Hyrcanus II even though he already had a wife and son. He hoped his marriage to a Jewish princess would win the people's approval, but he grossly miscalculated.

Herod lived on a tightrope. If he didn't please the Roman emperor, he could be removed from the throne. If he didn't please his people, they could revolt, which would upset the emperor. Herod trusted no one, not even his own family, and became increasingly paranoid as he aged. He executed his Jewish wife and three of his sons, murdering anyone he considered a threat.

When Herod heard about the caravan and the question being asked by Gentile magi, he summoned the chief priests and leading Torah teachers. "Where?" he demanded. "Where is the Messiah to be born?"

"Bethlehem," they answered.

Herod immediately sent for the magi and asked them when exactly they had first seen the star.

Mary and Joseph were still in Bethlehem when the star led the magi to them. The magi didn't arrive the night Jesus was born. Jesus is referred to as an infant (*brephos* in Greek) when the shepherds arrived, and as a child (*paidion*) when the wise men visited. The young parents might have been staying in the same house—though I assume they'd moved out of the animal pen—and would have remained in Bethlehem at least forty days, so Mary could visit the Temple for her purification ceremony.

They might have remained in Bethlehem for several months. Perhaps Joseph had undertaken a few jobs to earn his keep. Perhaps they were staying with relatives, since both their families had originally come from that town.

When the magi saw the star over the house, "they rejoiced exceedingly with great gladness. And when they came into the house, they saw the Child with His mother Miriam; and they fell down and worshiped Him. Then, opening their treasures, they presented to Him gifts of gold, frankincense, and myrrh. And having been warned in a dream not to go back to Herod, they returned to their own country by another way" (Matthew 2:10–12).

When the magi didn't return to Herod, he dispatched soldiers to kill every male baby in Bethlehem under two years of age, based on what the magi had told him about the appearance of the star. Though the slaughter of Bethlehem's baby boys isn't recorded in history, it is consistent with Herod's ruthless nature.

The prophecy can be found in Jeremiah 31:15, and in Matthew 2:18 we see the fulfillment: "A voice is heard in Ramah, weeping and loud wailing, Rachel sobbing for her children and refusing to be comforted, because they are no more."

This is another example of the law of double reference. When Jeremiah issued this prophecy, he referred to Rachel's sorrow as she died giving birth to Benjamin. She'd been on her way to Bethlehem (Ephrath) but died before reaching the city, so Jacob buried her at Ramah. Years later, at the beginning of the exile Jeremiah had predicted, Ramah was the city where Nebuzara-dan collected the Jews before marching them to Babylon. Jeremiah's prophecy evoked the image of Rachel lifting her head and weeping as the land emptied of her descendants, the Ephraimites.

In Matthew, the same prophecy refers to the weeping mothers of Bethlehem, Rachel's original destination, because Herod had killed their babies.

We don't know what became of the magi after they returned to their country. We don't know if meeting the infant Jesus had a lasting effect on their lives, but I believe it did. I can't imagine going through the journey, the encounter, and the rejoicing without being profoundly changed.

A Moment for Wonder

This story juxtaposes a religious pretender with pagan Gentiles. Both parties sought the newborn King of the Jews, but for completely different reasons. Herod possessed wealth and power, yet his ambition ruled his heart. He sought the King with a closed fist, determined to eliminate any threat to his throne.

The magi possessed the wealth and power of influential men, but their hearts were open to awe, wonder, and worship. They arrived with open hands and gifts that would provision Joseph and his family as they fled to Egypt.

The magi's hearts were set on worship, whereas Herod's heart was set on murder. A stark difference existed between the two, but even today some people worship the infant King, while others seem determined to quash every mention of His name.

Father, the difference between those who seek Jesus and those who want to deny His influence is particularly noticeable at Christmas. Help us be a witness for your Son in all that we say and do during this festive season. Remind us to provision those in need. Remind us that Christmas is not about power or wealth; it's about seeking, worshiping, and giving. We cannot give anything you have not given us, so help us to share your gifts with others. Fill our words with grace, and our hearts with gratitude.

FAMILY ACTIVITY FOR THE ADVENT SEASON

The People: The Menorah

If your family doesn't own a menorah, why not purchase or borrow one for this night? Though a Jewish family will light the menorah's candles on successive nights of Hanukkah, one candle for each night, you may want to light all the candles on one night.

A traditional menorah has holders for nine candles. Light the candles after dark so the flames can throw the greatest possible light.

A parent should light the center candle first. As you light it, explain that it is the *shamash* (sha-MAWSH), or helper candle, and represents God, who worked His purpose in the lives of the people we have read about.

Each candle represents someone who played a role in the birth of Christ. As the helper candle burns, use it to light the candles from the outside in on each side. As you light each candle, briefly describe this person's role in the Nativity story.

1. **Judah Maccabee:** He refused to obey the king, who wanted the Jews to forget God. If God hadn't used Judah and his brothers to resist the Seleucid king, Israel might not have existed as a separate people when Messiah was born.

2. **Zechariah and Elizabeth:** God put Zechariah in the right place at the right time and told him his son would help prepare the way of the Lord (Luke 1). In Elizabeth's old

age, she gave birth to John the Baptist. While her son was still in her womb, he recognized Mary's voice when she came to visit (Luke 1:44).

3. **Mary:** Gabriel visited her in Nazareth and told her she would have a baby to be named Jesus, meaning *salvation*. Her Son wouldn't have a biological father but would be miraculously conceived by the Holy Spirit (Luke 1:35).

4. **Joseph:** Joseph was engaged to Mary. When he heard she was pregnant, knowing he wasn't the father, he thought about divorcing her, but God sent an angel to assure him that the coming baby was a miraculous part of God's plan (Matthew 1:19).

5. **The Family**: We don't know their names, but a family in Bethlehem invited Mary and Joseph to spend the night in their animal shelter. Through their hospitality, God arranged a safe place for baby Jesus to be born.

6. **The Shepherds:** The shepherds were lowly people and usually avoided by others, yet they were the first to hear the angelic birth announcement (Luke 2:8).

7. **Simeon and Anna:** They were the first in the Temple to recognize the infant Jesus as Messiah. They had spent years praying and waiting for the Lord's promised Deliverer.

8. **The Magi and Herod:** The magi were Gentiles from the East. They knew a star would announce the birth of Israel's coming King. They recognized it and traveled west but didn't arrive until after the baby had been born. Then they gave Him gifts and worshiped Him.

When all the candles have been lit, ask one of the children to describe the role of each character again.

Pray together, thanking God for the willingness of so many people to do what God led them to do. Ask the Lord to show you and your family what He would like you to do during this holiday season.

PART 4

THE PURPOSE OF CHRISTMAS

21

IF CHRISTMAS
HAD NOT COME

I do not know whether an animal killed at Christmas has had a better or a worse time than it would have had if there had been no Christmas or no Christmas dinners. But I do know that the fighting and suffering brotherhood to which I belong and owe everything, mankind, would have a much worse time if there were no such thing as Christmas or Christmas dinners.

G. K. Chesterton (1874–1936)

The world has hope because Jesus came at Christmas.

If Jesus had not come, the abolition of slavery and the concept of equal rights among us would have occurred much later, if at all.

If Jesus had not come into the disciples' lives, they would have remained ordinary fishermen, tax collectors, and rebels. Instead, they became courageous miracle workers who revolutionized the world.

If Jesus had not come, the world would never have known the goodness of deeds done in His name. Charity hospitals, Christian relief efforts, and many other benevolent works would not exist.

If Jesus had not come, we would never know how much God loves us. The creation testifies of God's power, but Jesus testified of the Father's love.

If Jesus had not come, we would never have the assurance of eternal life. We would live and die, and our souls would spend eternity separated from God.

If Jesus had not come, we would have valid reasons to fear illness, death, poverty, and every sort of wickedness.

If Jesus had not come, we would never find release from our sinful natures. We would remain subject to our weaknesses and our sins.

If Jesus had not come, no one would be able to enjoy salvation. Only through His perfect life and sacrifice can we approach a holy God.

If Jesus had not come, we would have no opportunity to become children of God. That ability doesn't come from us, but from God alone.

If Jesus had not been born in Bethlehem, He would not be the Messiah because the prophet said the Messiah would be born in Bethlehem. This and myriad other prophecies have established who and what He was.

If Jesus had not been born of a virgin, He would be the child of an ordinary man and woman and therefore could not be fully God and perfect man. He would not have been the holy, innocent sacrifice for the sins of the world.

If Jesus had not come to show us the Father, we could be worshiping ancient gods. If we set aside the idea of divine gods, we would be worshiping at the altar of humanism, ascribing to ourselves the qualities of God. The wisest among us would realize that human perfection is an unattainable and even laughable concept.

If Jesus had not come, we would have no hope for this life or the life to come.

A Moment for Wonder

What would *your* world be like if Jesus had not come?

Today a Treasure is born to us.

Today the lantern of the virgin, kindled by the Holy Ghost, has manifested True Light.

Today the Physician of the blind is born.

Today the Health of the infirm.

Today the Strength of those that are weak, the Healing of those that are sick.

Today the Resurrection of the dead, our Savior, comes.

Today a new Light has appeared to us in the starry night.

Today our Savior approaches, whom the prophets had foretold, that He should be born of the virgin Mary.

Today the everlasting Bread of Light is shown to us, lying in a manger, who said, "I am the true Bread: if any man eat of this Bread he shall never hunger."

Grant us, Lord, by the virtue of your Nativity, to be freed from our ills and to glory in your praises.[1]

22

TO DEFEAT SIN

God gave us Christmas to defeat sin and our sin nature.

> So then, just as sin came into the world through one man and death through sin, in the same way death spread to all men because all sinned.
>
> Romans 5:12

Friends of mine recently had their first baby. As my husband and I smiled at the little boy's photos, I whispered, "Have you ever seen such innocence?"

The newborn child is not a sinner—one who has *purposely* disobeyed—but he was born with a sinful nature into a sinful world, and *as a sinner* his mother conceived him. Every mortal who lives will eventually sin because we cannot escape what we are unless and until we're born again and the Holy Spirit is allowed complete control of our lives.

David wrote Psalm 51 after his adultery with Bathsheba resulted in the death of their newborn son. The psalm records his anguish over his sin, and in verse seven we read, "Behold, I was born in iniquity and in sin when my mother conceived me."

When David's infant son died, David rose after praying, changed out of his mourning clothes, bathed, and went to worship in the house of the Lord. Then he ate dinner.

When his servants asked why he wasn't mourning the baby's death, David said, "While the child was yet alive, I fasted and wept, for I thought, 'Who knows? ADONAI might be gracious to me and let the child live.' But now that he has died, why should I fast? Can I bring him back again? It is I who will be going to him, but he will never return to me" (2 Samuel 12:22–23).

Though that baby was born with a sin nature, he never sinned, and David knew he would join him in heaven for eternity.

Some people read Romans 5:12 and conclude that because Adam sinned, all other humans are sinners *from birth*. But if babies are born with inherited sinful *deeds*, wouldn't Jesus have been born in a corrupted condition? His Father was God, but Mary was as human as we are. To get around this problem, some theologians have fashioned a doctrine stating that Mary was born without inherited sin, but weren't her parents sinners? And her grandparents?

There's a difference between willfully *committing sin* (acting in disobedience to God) and *having a sin nature* (a tendency to choose sin over obedience). The difference is similar to the concept of temptation: being tempted to sin is not sinful. Everyone experiences temptation, as did Jesus who was fully human. But sin doesn't occur until a person surrenders to that temptation.

I believe that Jesus, like other human babies, was born from a mother with a sinful human nature. In her lovely praise song, Mary said:

> "My soul magnifies the ADONAI,
> And my spirit greatly rejoices in God, my Savior.
> For He has looked with care upon the humble state of
>   His maidservant.
> For behold, from now on all generations will call me
>   blessed. . . ."

Luke 1:46–48

In her hymn of praise, Mary confesses that she is rejoicing in God her *Savior*, acknowledging her need for salvation.

Let's look more closely at Romans 5:12. Sin came into God's perfect world through the disobedient act of one man, Adam. The day Adam sinned, God told Adam he would die. Because of Adam's sin, *death* spread to all humans. Even Jesus experienced death as a result of sin—Adam's, not His. Jesus' human body died on the cross, and after the resurrection He walked and talked and ate in a supernatural resurrected body.

We are not born *sinners* (individuals who have disobeyed God); we are born with a *sin nature*. Left to follow our own desires, we will eventually sin.

A few years ago, I decided to raise chickens. I hatched several batches of eggs and was fascinated by the way the chicks developed. Did you know that baby chicks are fundamentally different from songbirds? No mama bird has to feed baby chicks. A hen doesn't have to teach them to scratch for food or bathe in sand to keep clean. Baby chicks can and will do such things after hatching because it's their *nature*. Chickens scratch and dust-bathe and peck because that's what chickens do.

Sin is an instinct of human nature. We don't *have* to sin, but our strong desire for self-preservation usually leads to lying or cheating even in early childhood. Break Mama's vase? Blame it on the dog. Sinning comes as naturally as breathing.

Was Jesus born with a sin nature? It feels blasphemous to think He was because He was the perfect, sinless sacrifice required to atone for our sin. Yet he had a human mother and was tempted by the devil, and can one be tempted if one has no desire for whatever's being offered?

Scripture leads me to believe that Jesus was born with the same free will and tendency toward sin that you and I were born with. Which makes His resistance to temptation—not only on one occasion but throughout His life—all the more amazing.

If He was born with a sin nature like all other people, He never once surrendered to sin, even as a child. He lived a full human life without sinning when He was tempted in the wilderness, overturned the money changers' tables, and when He prayed, "Father, if You are willing, take this cup from Me . . ." (Luke 22:42).

Scripture teaches that Jesus was fully God and perfect man without sin. "In the days of His life on earth, Yeshua offered up both prayers and pleas, with loud crying and tears, to the One able to save Him from death; and He was heard because of His reverence. Though He was a Son, He learned obedience from what He suffered" (Hebrews 5:7–8).

When did Jesus offer those prayers and pleas? *In the days of His life on earth*, He prayed and pleaded with God not only before the crucifixion but also throughout His life. He suffered through temptation just as we do, and He withstood the tempter every time, obeying His Father without fail.

"For we do not have a *kohen gadol* [high priest] who is unable to sympathize with our weaknesses, but One who *has been tempted in all the same ways*—yet without sin" (Hebrews 4:15, emphasis added).

Have you ever wondered why Jesus prayed so fervently in Gethsemane? Why would He ask for the "cup" to be taken away? Did He fear the physical pain of crucifixion? Did He dread the public humiliation involved? Was He having second thoughts?

I don't think Jesus dreaded any of those things. After all, He had fasted for forty days, so He was well acquainted with physical suffering.

The idea of sacrifice wasn't new to Him because God announced His plan for salvation in the Garden of Eden. In celebrating Yom Kippur, that plan was symbolized year after year as the high priest placed the sins of the people on a sacrificial scapegoat.

Jesus didn't worry about humiliation. He had already been mocked again and again by religious leaders, kings, and common folks. He'd been betrayed by people who loved Him.

I believe that Jesus prayed for the cup to be taken away because He flinched from the *effect* of the world's sin being laid on His shoulders. Sin separates us from God, and for a brief time, the Son, who had always been one with the Father, would have to endure that agonizing experience.

A Moment for Wonder

How could Jesus understand the power of temptation if He had no desire to sin? He was fully human. He hungered, He thirsted, He grew weary. He thought girls were pretty. He watched evil people prosper, and His fists clenched when He felt righteous anger, but even then, *He didn't sin.*

Through Jesus' life, death, and resurrection, He defeated Satan's plan for the corruption of the human race. Jesus also defeated the inherited sin nature. And knowing that God sent His Son to be tempted just like we are should only make us love and appreciate Him more.

> For if we have become joined together in the likeness of His death, certainly we also will be joined together in His resurrection—knowing our old man [the sin nature] was crucified with Him so that the sinful body might be done away with, so we no longer serve sin. For he who has died is set free from sin.
>
> Romans 6:5–7

Our sin nature—that desire for comfort, pleasure, and the things of this temporary world—will not exist in our resurrected bodies. This wonderful victory wouldn't have been possible if Jesus had not come to live a human life. Thank heaven for Christmas!

Father, help us to heed the Spirit, not the sin nature that in-dwells our mortal flesh. As Paul wrote, "Who will rescue me from this body of death? Thanks be to God—it is through Messiah Yeshua our Lord!"

Some days we feel like Jekyll and Hyde, wanting to do right, but finding it easier to do wrong . . . or to do nothing. Thank you, Father, for sending Jesus in human form so He could understand our struggles. Thank you for giving Him the strength to withstand every temptation from childhood to the cross. Remind us of His example when we are tempted and give us the strength to seek and do your will every time we must make a decision.

23

TO BRING US TO GOD

God gave us Christmas so that we could *reach* the One who created us.

> Thomas said to Him, "Master, we don't know where You are going. How can we know the way?"
> Yeshua said to him, "I am the way, the truth, and the life! No one comes to the Father except through Me. If you have come to know Me, you will know My Father also. From now on, you do know Him and have seen Him."
>
> John 14:5–7

"We realize," wrote Patrick Lumbroso, "that from the time Adam and Eve lost their place in the presence of Adonai in the Garden of Eden until today, no sinful natural man approaches HaShem [the Name] directly; it is always done through some sort of agency. Even though he appeared and was represented through many different venues before his ultimate manifestation 2,000 years ago, Messiah was, is, and will always be the quintessential agent through whom we approach the Father. Yeshua's own words, 'No man cometh unto the Father, but by me,' represent a fundamental truth prepared at the foundation of the world for all humanity from the days of Adam and Eve until now. . . . From eternity to eternity, it is through and in him that we approach HaShem."[1]

A recent study by Lifeway Research revealed that though nearly three in four Americans believe Jesus was born in Bethlehem more than two thousand years ago, less than half believe Jesus existed prior to being born. Many assume that since Jesus had an earthly mother and God as His father, He was half man and half God, but that isn't true.

But doesn't the Bible say Jesus was the "only begotten" of God? Doesn't that imply that He was created?

Michael Heiser explains why this is not the case:

> The Greek word translated by this phrase is *monogenes*. It doesn't mean "only begotten" in some sort of "birthing" sense. The confusion extends from an old misunderstanding of the root of the Greek word. For years monogenes was thought to have derived from two Greek terms, *monos* ("only") and *gennao* ("to beget, bear"). Greek scholars later discovered that the second part of the word monogenes does not come from the Greek verb gennao, but rather from the noun *genos* ("class, kind"). The term literally means "one of a kind" or "unique" without connotation of created origin.[2]

Yes, Jesus came to earth at Bethlehem, but He had visited men before. The Son of God, the unique second person of the Trinity, has always had a *supernatural* body—a body that can appear and disappear, just as He did after the resurrection when He joined

His disciples in the locked upper room (John 20:19). At His Nativity, that body was made tangible, and His mortal flesh concealed the brightness of His glory. Only once, during the transfiguration, did His glory shine through.[3]

Jesus came to us . . . to bring us to God.

When we observe Christmas, our reason for celebration shouldn't be limited to the miraculous arrival of the virgin-born baby. The Nativity encompasses so much more! We should be unspeakably grateful that the second person of the Trinity was willing to leave heaven and live among us.

The baby born in Bethlehem, a child fully God and perfect man, was God's preordained sacrifice for the sins of the world.

Every year the Jewish high priest sacrificed animals to cover his sins, as well as those of his family and Israel. But the practice of sacrificing animals to pay for sin became obsolete when Messiah offered His sinless mortal body as the sacrifice. He felt the bite of the nails and the agony of snapping tendons. He suffered mentally, emotionally, and physically so we could be forgiven, not on an annual basis through sacrifice, but for all time.

> In the days of His life on earth, Yeshua offered up both prayers and pleas, with loud crying and tears, to the One able to save Him from death; and He was heard because of His reverence. Though He was a Son, He learned obedience from what He suffered. And once made perfect, He became the source of eternal salvation to all who obey Him—called by God *Kohen Gadol* [High Priest] "according to the order of Melchizedek."
>
> Hebrews 5:7–10 (see also Psalm 110:4)

So when Messiah comes into the world, He says,

"Sacrifice and offering You did not desire, but a body You prepared for Me. In whole burnt offerings and sin offerings You did not delight. Then I said, 'Behold, I come to do Your will, O God (in the scroll of the book it is written of Me).'"

After saying above, "Sacrifices and offerings and whole burnt offerings and sin offerings You did not desire, nor did You delight in them" (those which are offered according to *Torah*), then He said, "Behold, I come to do Your will." He takes away the first to establish the second. By His will we have been made holy through the offering of the body of Messiah *Yeshua* once for all.

Hebrews 10:5–10

God often reveals truths in signs, and several occurred during Christ's crucifixion. One was the tearing of the veil that separated the Holy of Holies from the Temple court. The thick, thirty-foot-long curtain ripped from top to bottom, indicating a new and direct way to approach God (Matthew 27:51).

Therefore, brothers and sisters, we have boldness to enter into the Holies by the blood of Yeshua. He inaugurated a new and living way for us through the curtain—that is, His flesh. We also have a Kohen Gadol over God's household.

So let us draw near with a true heart in full assurance of faith, with hearts sprinkled clean from an evil conscience and body washed with pure water.

Let us hold fast the unwavering confession of hope, for He who promised is faithful.

Hebrews 10:19–23

Several other odd events happened in AD 30, the probable year of Christ's crucifixion. Though the rabbis recorded these anomalies, they didn't see any connection between Jesus' death and the establishment of a new way to draw near to God.

Forty years before the destruction of the Temple, the rabbis wrote, the heavy Temple gates, which were always closed, swung open of their own accord. That same year, the lintel of the Temple broke and fell.

Josephus mentions that during this same year, the chief light in the golden lampstand inexplicably went out.

As I've already mentioned, AD 30 was also the year in which the scapegoat's sash didn't turn white.

When Jesus died, He uttered one last word, rendered in Greek as *"Tetelestai."* This word has been found on ancient receipts to indicate that a debt had been paid in full. Most Bibles translate the word to mean *It is finished*, but the Greek implies a deeper meaning. Our debt—our sin debt—was paid in full. The chasm between humanity and God had been bridged.

Gabriel told Mary to name her son *Yeshua*, the word used by Moses and the prophets whenever they wrote of salvation. When the Jews read the psalms and the prophets, they read the name of Messiah over and over again.

Consider Isaiah 12:2–3 in English:

> "Behold, God is my salvation!
> I will trust and will not be afraid.
> For the Lord ADONAI is my strength and my song.
> He also has become my salvation."

> With joy you will draw water
> from the wells of salvation.

Now read the same Scripture but with Hebrew words:

> Hinei, El is my **Yeshuah**;
> I will trust, and not be afraid;
> for HaShem G-d is my strength and my zemirah;
> He also has become my **Yeshuah**.
> Therefore with sasson shall ye draw mayim
> out of the wells of **Yeshuah**.
>
> Isaiah 12:2–3 OJB

For generations, the truth was predicted and revealed in Scripture—salvation would be found in Yeshua. Gabriel told Mary to name her Son *salvation* because His birth, life, and sacrificial death were ordained before time began.

The story of Jesus didn't begin with His conception or the baby in the manger. His story has no beginning at all.

A Moment for Wonder

Yeshua is the name above every name. He is the Living Water, the Bread of Life, the Light of the World, the Son of God, the Son of Man, the Good Shepherd, the Vine, the Door, the Way, the Word, the Word Made Flesh, the Last Adam, the Image of the Invisible God, the Firstborn over All Creation, the Lion of the Tribe of Judah, the Servant of the Lord, the Righteous Branch, the Root of Jesse, the Way, the Truth, and the Life. He is the Alpha and the Omega, the Bright and Morning Star. He is the Rock and the Cornerstone of God's plan for human beings.

He is Immanuel, God with us.

He is the Lamb of God, intended for sacrifice and victory over sin and death.

Each name portrays a different facet of Jesus, but His name encompasses everything He is. He is salvation for lost men and women, misguided nations, and a corrupted universe.

If you are lost, Yeshua is hope. If you are unhappy, He is joy. If you are weary, He is rest. If you are guilty—and we all are—His blood has secured our pardon.

He is Yeshua, Jesus, our way to God in this life and the Giver of eternal life to come.

Father, we cannot see your likeness now, but one day we will. Instead, you gave us your Son, so we pray in His name, do good works in His name, praise His name, and are forgiven in His name. We approach you through His name. Help us remember never to carry His name lightly or irreverently, but to be always conscious that we bear His name in a world desperate for healing light.

How we thank you for sending Jesus to fulfill the needs of fallen people. Thank you that He made a way for us to draw near to your throne of grace. Hasten the day when every knee shall bow at the name of your precious Son, Yeshua Messiah.

24

TO BRING GOD TO US

God gave us Christmas because He wants to live with us just as He did with Adam and Eve. Since man's disobedience in the garden, God has been reaching out to His errant people. He has displayed His art and majesty in creation. He has demonstrated His power in thundering storms. He has confirmed His goodness with the common grace that guides all those of goodwill.

He proved His great love by sending Jesus.

> Philip said to Him, "Master, show us the Father, and it is enough for us."
>
> Yeshua said to him, "Have I been with you for so long a time, and you haven't come to know Me, Philip? He who has seen Me has seen the Father. . . ."
>
> John 14:8–9

No sinful human can look upon the full glory of a holy God and live. Moses, however, was able to look upon God's likeness and talk with Him face-to-face. How? He spoke with the preincarnate Messiah, the *temunah* or likeness of God.

The Lord assured Aaron and Miriam that Moses had seen His likeness:

> "When there is a prophet of ADONAI, I reveal Myself in a vision,
> I speak to him in a dream. Not so with My servant Moses. In all
> My house, he is faithful. I speak with him face to face, plainly and
> not in riddles. He even looks at the form [*temunah*] of ADONAI!"
>
> Numbers 12:6–8

The Old Testament refers to the preincarnate Jesus not only as the temunah but also as *Malach panav*, the *Memra*, and the "Angel of the Lord." Christian theologians call such an appearance a *theophany*. John spoke of Jesus as *the Word*:

> In the beginning was the Word. The Word was with God, and the
> Word was God. He was with God in the beginning. All things were
> made through Him, and apart from Him nothing was made that
> has come into being.
>
> John 1:1–3

The Old Testament is sprinkled with mentions of the preexistent Christ, demonstrating that He came to us on several occasions. Abraham entertained two angels as well as the Angel of the Lord, then knelt and worshiped Him (Genesis 18).

Who can forget the heartrending story of Abraham journeying to Mount Moriah to offer Isaac, his beloved son, as a sacrifice? Just as Abraham was about to strike the fatal blow,

> The angel of ADONAI called to Abraham a second time from heaven
> and said, "*By myself I swear*—it is a *declaration of ADONAI*—because

you have done this thing, and you did not withhold your son, your only son, I will richly bless you and bountifully multiply your seed like the stars of heaven, and like the sand that is on the seashore, and your seed will possess the gate of his enemies. In your seed all the nations of the earth will be blessed—because you obeyed My voice."

Genesis 22:15–18 (italics added)

The Angel of Adonai speaks *for* Adonai and *with* Adonai. This Angel is the preincarnate Messiah.

The Old Testament tells us about the Angel of the Lord appearing to Jacob, Isaac, Moses, and Gideon. We see Him walking through fire with Shadrach, Meshach, and Abednego.

The Angel of the Lord appeared to Samson's parents and ascended in the flame of their sacrifice (Judges 13).

The preincarnate Messiah did far more than deliver messages and accept worship. He also led Israel out of Egypt and destroyed their enemies:

"Behold, I am going to send an Angel before you to keep and guard you on the way and to bring you to the place I have prepared. Be on your guard before Him, listen to and obey His voice; do not be rebellious toward Him or provoke Him, for He will not pardon your transgression, since My Name (authority) is in Him. But if you will indeed listen to and truly obey His voice and do everything that I say, then I will be an enemy to your enemies and an adversary to your adversaries. When My Angel goes before you and brings you to [the land of] the Amorite, the Hittite, the Perizzite, the Canaanite, the Hivite, and the Jebusite, I

will reject them and completely destroy them. You shall not bow
down to worship their gods, nor serve them, nor do [anything] in
accordance with their practices. You shall completely overthrow
them and break down their [sacred] pillars and images [of pagan
worship]. . . ."

Exodus 23:20–24 AMP

Now I want to remind you, although you once fully knew it, that
Jesus, who saved a people out of the land of Egypt, afterward destroyed those who did not believe.

Jude 5 ESV

How could the Jews, who every morning and night recited,
"Hear O Israel, the LORD our God, the LORD is one" (Deuteronomy 6:4), accept the idea that God, Jesus, and the Spirit were
separate persons and still one God? Not all the Jews could, and
many still struggle with this concept. But the Hebrew text makes
it clear: "*Shema Yisroel Adonai Eloheinu Adonai Echad.*" The Hebrew word *echad* means one in nature, a compound unity. Elo-
him. A plural God.

The Torah teachers said that though the entire earth wasn't
large enough to contain God's glory, He could concentrate His
being to fill one small space—the Tabernacle, for instance, or
the Temple.

So why not a human body?

The idea of the Trinity—one God in three eternal, inseparable
persons—is difficult to comprehend, though many have tried to
come up with a suitable metaphor. An egg has three parts—white,

yolk, and shell—but fails as an analogy for the Godhead because an egg can be separated and God cannot. Water, too, consists of three forms—solid, liquid, and steam—but water cannot exist in all three forms simultaneously as God does.

God is three equal persons—Father, Son, and Spirit—though the Son and Spirit willingly submit to the Father. We may not be able to understand how such a paradox exists, but the Scriptures illustrate that it does.

John 1:1–3 tells us that Jesus, the Word, was present at creation, and "All things were made through Him, and apart from Him nothing was made." All three members of the Godhead created our world even though God knew Adam and Eve would sin, even though He knew a perfect sacrifice would be required to redeem fallen humanity and restore the earth.

After the Nativity, Jesus possessed a vulnerable human body. He hungered. He bled. He suffered pain. He got the sniffles and coughed and grew weary, and when He had completed the work He was sent to do,

> He humbled Himself—
> becoming obedient to the point of death,
> even death on a cross.
>
> Philippians 2:8

Christmas—all the events surrounding the birth of the Savior God promised to Adam and Eve—was the most anticipated move in God's redemptive plan.

A Moment for Wonder

Why did God send Jesus? Because He wants to live with us in the new Heaven and on the new Earth.

Michael Heiser explains:

> What was ruined by the fall is restored—and made irreversible—by the incarnation of Yahweh [Jesus], his atoning death, and his resurrection. But all that is relatively easy to talk about when compared to passages that deal with what comes last and remains forever.
>
> How do you describe the indescribable? Paul grasped the problem clearly. I still like the King James Version of his sentiments for their rhythmic, almost lyrical quality: "Eye hath not seen, nor ear heard, neither have entered into the heart of man, the things which God hath prepared for them that love him" (1 Corinthians 2:9).[1]

The Son of God, who was present at creation, ate dinner with Moses and the elders of Israel, spoke with Abraham, wrestled with Jacob, and strolled with three Hebrew exiles in a right royal furnace. This same Messiah humbled himself to be born as a baby to humble people in a humble setting. He did these things so He could live with us—fellowship with us, laugh and dine and reason with us.

Astounding, isn't it?

Father, throughout history you provided human mediators such as Moses, the prophets, kings, and high priests of Israel, but only Christ was able to bridge the divide that separates our sinful selves from your holiness. He alone had the ability to usher us, redeemed and renewed, into your holy presence.

We can't begin to grasp what you have planned for the new Heaven and new Earth. The thought that you would do so much for us boggles the mind. This Christmas help us to appreciate all that you have done, and all you have planned for eternity.

25

SO WE WOULD HAVE COURAGE

God gave us Christmas so we could be courageous in everything we do.

A few years ago, I decided to write a series of novels about life in a funeral home. When I announced my intention, I was amazed that some readers were repulsed by the idea because they didn't want to think about death. Why should we Christians—for whom eternal life with Jesus is a certain promise—be afraid to die? Why should we be afraid of *anything*?

The story of Jesus is punctuated with an admonition: "Fear not!" When God works, some may be scared speechless, but we are not to fear because our sovereign God is *always* in control.

Zechariah may have been terrified when the angel arrived, yet he had no cause for fear: "But the angel said, '**Do not be afraid**, Zechariah, because your prayer has been heard. Your wife, Elizabeth, will give birth to your son, and you will name him John'" (Luke 1:13).

Mary was undoubtedly startled when Gabriel appeared, but she had no reason to fear: "The angel spoke to her, '**Do not be afraid**, Miriam, for you have found favor with God. Behold, you will become pregnant and give birth to a son, and you shall call His name Yeshua'" (Luke 1:30–31).

Joseph didn't know what to do about his pregnant fiancée, but assurance soon arrived: "Behold, an angel of ADONAI appeared to him in a dream, saying, 'Joseph son of David, **do not be afraid** to take Miriam as your wife, for the Child conceived in her is from the Ruach ha-Kodesh [the Holy Spirit]'" (Matthew 1:20).

The shepherds stared in astonished wonder, but the messenger brought an amazing report: "But the angel said to them, '**Do not be afraid!** For behold, I proclaim Good News to you, which will be great joy to all the people. A Savior is born to you today in the city of David, who is Messiah the Lord'" (Luke 2:10–11).

Simon Peter must have thought he was dreaming when his nets broke from the weight of so many fish, but Jesus assured him that he hadn't seen anything yet: "'**Do not be afraid.** From now on, you will be catching men'" (Luke 5:10).

The worried father was terrified at the thought of losing his precious daughter, but Jesus gave him peace: "'**Do not fear**—just keep trusting, and she shall be restored'" (Luke 8:50).

We tend to worry about all sorts of things, but Jesus assured us that God has every part of our lives under His control: "Indeed, even the hairs of your head are all numbered. So **do not fear**; you are more valuable than many sparrows" (Luke 12:7).

Children fear things they don't understand, so Jesus told us that God cares for us like a Father. He promises to provide all that we need if we trust Him: "**Do not be afraid**, little flock, for your Father chose to give you the kingdom" (Luke 12:32).

The people of Jerusalem lived in dread of Rome, with good reason, and they were desperate for relief. When Jesus entered Jerusalem the week before his death, Messianic fervor was at such a fevered pitch that the people shouted "Hosanna!" (*deliver us*) as He rode in. They *were* about to be delivered, but from sin—an enemy far more destructive than Rome: "Finding a young donkey, Yeshua sat on it, as it is written, '**Fear not**, Daughter of Zion! Look! Your King is coming, sitting on a donkey's colt'" (John 12:14–15; Zechariah 9:9).

Mary Magdalene and the other Mary went to Jesus' tomb and found it sealed and guarded. Then the earth trembled, and an angel as bright as lightning came down, rolled away the stone, and sat on it as if it were a mere plaything. The guards were so terrified they fainted. The women didn't.

"The angel answered and said to the women, '**Do not be afraid**, for I know you are looking for Yeshua who was crucified. He is not here; for He is risen, just as He said'" (Matthew 28:5–6).

Exiled on the island of Patmos because of his Christian testimony, John heard a sound like a trumpet and saw the resurrected, glorified Christ, who had a message for the Church:

In the midst of the *menorot* [menorahs], I saw One like a Son of Man, clothed in a robe down to His feet, with a golden belt wrapped around His chest. His head and His hair were white like wool, white like snow, and His eyes like a flame of fire. His feet were like polished bronze refined in a furnace, and His voice was like the roar of rushing waters. In His right hand He held seven stars, and out of His mouth came forth a sharp, two-edged sword. His face was like the sun shining at full strength.

When I saw Him, I fell at His feet like a dead man. But He placed His right hand on me, saying, "**Do not be afraid!** I am the First and the Last, and the One who lives. I was dead, but look—I am alive forever and ever! Moreover, I hold the keys of death and Sheol [the grave]. . . ."

Revelation 1:13–18

A Moment for Wonder

We are surrounded by a great cloud of invisible witnesses, the saints who displayed *parresia*, the Greek word translated as *boldness*, *courage*, and *confidence*. The believers who have gone before us displayed this courage when they publicly proclaimed the Gospel. Placing obedience to God before the opinions of men, they upheld God's truth, often at the risk of their lives.

They were also courageous in their prayers and the provision of other believers. They prayed in faith, believing God would answer. And they gave boldly, knowing God would take care of them when they provided for others.

A dear friend of mine likes to say that when God sent Jesus to earth, He didn't send the Savior off by saying "Take care!" Instead, God told His Son, "Take risks!"

Christmas is a time to forget about everything but one amazing miracle: God Almighty so loved this fallen world that He sent His Son to be born in vulnerable mortal flesh. Jesus had the courage to take risks, so why don't we?

Fear not, brothers and sisters in Christ! Tomorrow, resolve to live with courage even if you don't feel courageous. Take risks for the Lord, and don't worry. Your heavenly Father loves you, He cares for you, and He's willing to use your life in ways you can't even imagine.

Father, when we consider what the early believers endured because of their courageous words and deeds, we are challenged to live with faith and holy boldness. You sent your Son to live a courageous life, so remind us, Father, that we are not to fear anything. We give you our possessions, our families, our lives, and all our worries. Do with us as you will, fill us with your wisdom, and give us the courage and confidence to take risks!

FAMILY ACTIVITY FOR THE ADVENT SEASON

The Purpose: Your Family Traditions

This is likely to be a busy week, perhaps filled with travel, company, shopping, baking, and all sorts of holiday activities. Even so, try to find some time this week to sit and talk about your family traditions. What do you enjoy doing together? What motivates you to do this activity?

How do your traditions differ from the first Christmas in Bethlehem? What have you learned over the course of this book, and how can this knowledge help you appreciate and enjoy Christmas even more?

Angela Hunt has published more than 150 books, with sales exceeding five million copies worldwide. She's the *New York Times* bestselling author of *The Tale of Three Trees*, *The Note*, and *The Nativity Story*. Angela's novels have won or been nominated for several prestigious industry awards, such as the RITA Award, the Christy Award, the ECPA Christian Book Award, and the HOLT Medallion Award. Romantic Times Book Club presented her with a Lifetime Achievement Award in 2006. She holds doctorates in Biblical Studies and Theology. Angela and her husband live in Florida, along with their mastiffs and chickens. For a complete list of the author's books, visit angelahuntbooks.com.

NOTES

Chapter 1 Bethlehem

1. R. Gower and F. Wright, *The New Manners and Customs of Bible Times*, updated and rewritten version of *Manners and Customs of Bible Lands* by Fred Wright (Chicago: Moody Press, 1997).

Chapter 2 The Garden

1. Arnold G. Fruchtenbaum, *Yeshua: The Life of Messiah from a Messianic Jewish Perspective* (San Antonio, TX: Ariel Ministries, 2016), 1:296.

2. Santala, *The Messiah in the Old Testament in the Light of Rabbinical Writings*, 194–195, quoted by Arnold G. Fruchtenbaum, *Yeshua*, vol. 1, op. cit., 367.

Chapter 3 The Shepherd's Field

1. Edwin Firmage, "Zoology (Fauna): Animal Profiles," in *The Anchor Yale Bible Dictionary*, ed. David Noel Freedman (New Haven, CT: Yale University Press, 1992), 1,126.

2. Firmage, "Zoology."

Chapter 4 The Eastern Kingdom

1. Ancient people measured years differently than we do. Their calendar measured 12 lunar months of 30 days, making a year 360 days.

Chapter 5 The Temple

1. John E. Hartley, *Leviticus*, Word Biblical Commentary (Dallas: Word, Incorporated, 1992), vol. 4.

2. Fruchtenbaum, *Yeshua*, 1:421.

Chapter 6 Egypt

1. Albert Edersheim, *Bible History: Old Testament* (Grand Rapids, MI: William B. Eerdmans Publishing Co., 1975), vol. 1.

2. Seth Postell, Eitan Bar, and Erez Soref, *Reading Moses, Seeing Jesus: How the Torah Fulfills its Goal in Yeshua* (One for Israel Ministry, 2017).

Chapter 7 Nazareth

1. Steven R. Notley, "Matthew 2:1–23, A Nazorean Shall Be Called," Jerusalem Perspective, December 7, 2015, https://www.jerusalemperspective.com/15149/.

2. Earl D. Radmacher, Ronald Barclay Allen, and H. Wayne House, *The Nelson Study Bible: New King James Version* (Nashville, TN: Thomas Nelson Publishers, 1997).

3. Arnold G. Fruchtenbaum, *Yeshua: The Life of Messiah from a Messianic Jewish Perspective* (San Antonio, TX: Ariel Ministries, 2017), 2:136.

Chapter 8 Prophecies of the Coming Messiah

1. Lois Tverberg, *Reading the Bible with Rabbi Jesus* (Grand Rapids, MI: Baker Books, 2017), 201.

2. Arnold G. Fruchtenbaum, *The Messianic Bible Study Collection* (Tustin, CA: Ariel Ministries, 1983), vol. 12.

Chapter 9 Prophecies in Patterns

1. Fruchtenbaum, *Yeshua*, 1:376.

2. Ibid.

Chapter 10 Prophecies of Messiah's Lineage

1. Fruchtenbaum, *Yeshua*, op. cit., 280.

2. John C. Hutchison, "Women, Gentiles, and the Messianic Mission in Matthew's Genealogy," *Bibliotheca Sacra* 158, no. 630 (April–June 2002): 152–164.

Chapter 11 Prophecies of Timing

1. Arnold G. Fruchtenbaum, *Yeshua: The Life of Messiah from a Messianic Jewish Perspective* (San Antonio, TX: Ariel Ministries, 2020), 1:381.

2. Barney Kasdan, *The Seven Festivals of the Messiah* (Shippensburg, PA: Destiny Image Publishers, 1994), 177.

3. *Midrash Raba Bereshit*, parashah 56, quoted in Julia Blum's *If You Are the Son of God*, 39.

4. Julia Blum, *If You Are the Son of God* (self-pub., 2016), 154.

Chapter 12 Prophecies of Messiah's People

1. Dinesh D'Souza, "*Was Hitler a Christian?*" CERC, November 1, 2007, https://www.catholiceducation.org/en/controversy/common-misconceptions/was-hitler-a-christian.html.

Chapter 13 The Prophecy of Melchizedek

1. Robert B. Hughes and J. Carl Laney, *Tyndale Concise Bible Commentary* (Wheaton, IL: Tyndale House Publishers, 2001).

2. Alfred Edersheim, *The Temple: Its Ministry and Services as They Were at the Time of Jesus Christ* (London: James Clarke & Co., 1959).

3. Arnold G. Fruchtenbaum, *The Messianic Bible Study Collection* (Tustin, CA: Ariel Ministries, 1983), vol. 70.

4. Bob Larkin, "23 Hilarious Predictions about the Year 2020 that Are Way Off," December 8, 2019, https://bestlifeonline.com/2020-predictions/.

5. Ibid.

6. Ibid.
7. Ibid.
8. Ibid.

Chapter 15 Zechariah

1. Adapted from *The Nativity Story* by Angela Hunt and based on the screenplay by Mike Rich. Wheaton, IL: Tyndale House Publishers, 2006.

Chapter 16 John the Baptizer

1. Fruchtenbaum, *Yeshua*, 1:363.
2. Fruchtenbaum, *Yeshua*, 2:73.

Chapter 17 Mary of Nazareth

1. Fruchtenbaum, *Yeshua*, 1:329.

Chapter 18 Joseph the Builder

1. Paul H Wright, "The Size and Makeup of Nazareth at the Time of Jesus," in *Lexham Geographic Commentary on the Gospels*, eds. Barry J. Beitzel and Kristopher A. Lyle (Bellingham, WA: Lexham Press, 2016), 38–39.
2. Wright, "Nazareth at the Time of Jesus."

Chapter 19 The Shepherds and Angels

1. "Agriculture in Israel: History and Overview," Jewish Virtual Library, https://www.jewishvirtuallibrary.org/history-and-overview-of-agriculture-in-israel (accessed October 20, 2022).

Chapter 21 If Christmas Had Not Come

1. Elliot Ritzema, ed., *300 Quotations and Prayers for Christmas* (Bellingham, WA: Lexham Press, 2013).

Chapter 23 To Bring Us to God

1. Patrick Gabriel Lumbroso, *Under the Vine: Messianic Thought through the Hebrew Calendar* (Clarksville, MD: Lederer Books, a division of Messianic Jewish Publishers, 2013).
2. Michael S. Heiser, *The Unseen Realm: Recovering the Supernatural Worldview of the Bible* (Bellingham, WA: Lexham Press, 2015), loc. 591–597, Kindle.
3. Fruchtenbaum, *Yeshua*, 1:242.

Chapter 24 To Bring God to Us

1. Michael S. Heiser, *The Unseen Realm: Recovering the Supernatural Worldview of the Bible* (Bellingham, WA: Lexham Press, 2015).